MACMILLAN MASTER GUIDES

GENERAL EDITOR: JAMES GIBSON

JANE AUSTEN	*Emma* Norman Page
	Sense and Sensibility Judy Simons
	Persuasion Judy Simons
	Pride and Prejudice Raymond Wilson
	Mansfield Park Richard Wirdnam
SAMUEL BECKETT	*Waiting for Godot* Jennifer Birkett
WILLIAM BLAKE	*Songs of Innocence* and *Songs of Experience* Alan Tomlinson
ROBERT BOLT	*A Man for All Seasons* Leonard Smith
CHARLOTTE BRONTË	*Jane Eyre* Robert Miles
EMILY BRONTË	*Wuthering Heights* Hilda D. Spear
JOHN BUNYAN	*The Pilgrim's Progress* Beatrice Batson
GEOFFREY CHAUCER	*The Miller's Tale* Michael Alexander
	The Pardoner's Tale Geoffrey Lester
	The Wife of Bath's Tale Nicholas Marsh
	The Knight's Tale Anne Samson
	The Prologue to the Canterbury Tales Nigel Thomas and Richard Swan
JOSEPH CONRAD	*The Secret Agent* Andrew Mayne
CHARLES DICKENS	*Bleak House* Dennis Butts
	Great Expectations Dennis Butts
	Hard Times Norman Page
GEORGE ELIOT	*Middlemarch* Graham Handley
	Silas Marner Graham Handley
	The Mill on the Floss Helen Wheeler
T.S. ELIOT	*Murder in the Cathedral* Paul Lapworth
	Selected Poems Andrew Swarbrick
HENRY FIELDING	*Joseph Andrews* Trevor Johnson
E.M. FORSTER	*A Passage to India* Hilda D. Spear
	Howards End Ian Milligan
WILLIAM GOLDING	*The Spire* Rosemary Sumner
	Lord of the Flies Raymond Wilson
OLIVER GOLDSMITH	*She Stoops to Conquer* Paul Ranger
THOMAS HARDY	*The Mayor of Casterbridge* Ray Evans
	Tess of the d'Urbervilles James Gibson
	Far from the Madding Crowd Colin Temblett-Wood
BEN JONSON	*Volpone* Michael Stout
JOHN KEATS	*Selected Poems* John Garrett
RUDYARD KIPLING	*Kim* Leonée Ormond
PHILIP LARKIN	*The Less Deceived* and *The Whitsun Weddings* Andrew Swarbrick

MACMILLAN MASTER GUIDES

D. H. LAWRENCE	*Sons and Lovers* R. P. Draper
HARPER LEE	*To Kill a Mockingbird* Jean Armstrong
LAURIE LEE	*Cider with Rosie* Brian Tarbitt
GERARD MANLEY HOPKINS	*Selected Poems* R. J. C. Watt
CHRISTOPHER MARLOWE	*Doctor Faustus* David A. Male
THE METAPHYSICAL POETS	Joan van Emden
THOMAS MIDDLETON and WILLIAM ROWLEY	*The Changeling* Tony Bromham
ARTHUR MILLER	*The Crucible* Leonard Smith *Death of a Salesman* Peter Spalding
GEORGE ORWELL	*Animal Farm* Jean Armstrong
WILLIAM SHAKESPEARE	*Richard II* Charles Barber *Othello* Tony Bromham *Hamlet* Jean Brooks *King Lear* Francis Casey *Henry V* Peter Davison *The Winter's Tale* Diana Devlin *Julius Caesar* David Elloway *Macbeth* David Elloway *The Merchant of Venice* A. M. Kinghorn *Measure for Measure* Mark Lilly *Henry IV Part I* Helen Morris *Romeo and Juliet* Helen Morris *A Midsummer Night's Dream* Kenneth Pickering *The Tempest* Kenneth Pickering *Coriolanus* Gordon Williams *Antony and Cleopatra* Martin Wine
GEORGE BERNARD SHAW	*St Joan* Leonée Ormond
RICHARD SHERIDAN	*The School for Scandal* Paul Ranger *The Rivals* Jeremy Rowe
ALFRED TENNYSON	*In Memoriam* Richard Gill
EDWARD THOMAS	*Selected Poems* Gerald Roberts
ANTHONY TROLLOPE	*Barchester Towers* K. M. Newton
JOHN WEBSTER	*The White Devil* and *The Duchess of Malfi* David A. Male
VIRGINIA WOOLF	*To the Lighthouse* John Mepham *Mrs Dalloway* Julian Pattison
WILLIAM WORDSWORTH	*The Prelude Books I and II* Helen Wheeler

MACMILLAN MASTER GUIDES

THE LESS DECEIVED AND

THE WHITSUN WEDDINGS

BY PHILIP LARKIN

ANDREW SWARBRICK

MACMILLAN

First published 1986
Reprinted 1989, 1990

Published by
MACMILLAN EDUCATION LTD
Houndmills, Basingstoke, Hampshire RG21 2XS
and London
Companies and representatives
throughout the world

Printed in Hong Kong

British Library Cataloguing in Publication Data
Swarbrick, Andrew
The less deceived and The Whitsun weddings.–
(Macmillan master guides).
1. Larkin, Philip. Less deceived   2. Larkin,
Philip. Whitsun weddings
I. Title
821'.914   PR6023.A66L4
ISBN 0-333-41714-3 Pbk
ISBN 0-333-41715-1 Pbk export

CONTENTS

GENERAL EDITOR'S PREFACE

The aim of the Macmillan Master Guides is to help you to appreciate the book you are studying by providing information about it and by suggesting ways of reading and thinking about it which will lead to a fuller understanding. The section on the writer's life and background has been designed to illustrate those aspects of the writer's life which have influenced the work, and to place it in its personal and literary context. The summaries and critical commentary are of special importance in that each brief summary of the action is followed by an examination of the significant critical points. The space which might have been given to repetitive explanatory notes has been devoted to a detailed analysis of the kind of passage which might confront you in an examination. Literary criticism is concerned with both the broader aspects of the work being studied and with its detail. The ideas which meet us in reading a great work of literature, and their relevance to us today, are an essential part of our study, and our Guides look at the thought of their subject in some detail. But just as essential is the craft with which the writer has constructed his work of art, and this may be considered under several technical headings – characterisation, language, style and stagecraft, for example.

The authors of these Guides are all teachers and writers of wide experience, and they have chosen to write about books they admire and know well in the belief that they can communicate their admiration to you. But you yourself must read and know intimately the book you are studying. No one can do that for you. You should see this book as a lamp-post. Use it to shed light, not to lean against. If you know your text and know what it is saying about life, and how it says it, then you will enjoy it, and there is no better way of passing an examination in literature.

JAMES GIBSON

ACKNOWLEDGEMENTS

Cover illustration: *An Island* by L. S. Lowry, 1942. © Manchester City Art Gallery and by courtesy of the Bridgeman Art Library.

The author and publishers wish to thank the following who have kindly given permission for the use of copyright material; Faber & Faber Ltd for extracts from *The Whitsun Weddings* by Philip Larkin; The Marvell Press for extracts from *The Less Deceived* by Philip Larkin.

Every effort has been made to trace all the copyright-holders, but if any have been inadvertently overlooked the publishers will be pleased to make the necessary arrangement at the first opportunity.

1 PHILIP LARKIN:
LIFE AND BACKGROUND

A critical study of Philip Larkin's poetry - even such a slim and modest one as this - treads on thin ice. Larkin's poems hardly need explication for they offer themselves with such an easy grace and clarity that the critic is rightly made redundant by them. Larkin's aim was to address himself to readers, not to the lit. crit. industry, and he expresses himself with a directness and eloquence which should have no need of the intermediary services of the critic. What necessity, then, for a survey such as this? First, because we are usually so lazy in our reading that we need to be reminded that poems demand a different sort of attention. Reading poems is an activity different from reading, say, a newspaper report or popular fiction. We have to be much more alert to words and the way they are used and this simple fact has been so obscured that we need to remind ourselves of it by books such as this. Secondly, Larkin's poems are so eminently *readable* that it is particularly easy to overlook their craft and artistry: Larkin has the gift of making the highly complex activity of poetry look so easy that his real mastery is in danger of being passed over. But you must remember that what is presented here is only an introduction to the poems, brief sketches which you need to amplify by your own close reading. This survey can only help you to your own fuller understanding of Larkin's poetry by encouraging you to explore it further on your own.

Philip Larkin was born in Coventry, an industrial Midlands town, in 1922. His father was city treasurer and Larkin was born into an orthodox professional background. His childhood was uneventful and unmemorable and Larkin later characterised it as 'a forgotten boredom'; in 'I Remember, I Remember' he wittily debunks the romantic clichés popularly associated with childhood and adolescence. He claimed not to have been particularly successful at school, dull at everything except English, and resentful of its intrusions on his private fantasies and daydreams. 'A Study of Reading Habits' shows his voracious appetite for escapist reading of the usual kind, but his father's library offered modern writers such as D. H. Lawrence and Aldous Huxley who were considered rather daring in their time. In his mid-teens, Larkin followed a strict régime of writing prose and verse, most of which went unpublished, and developed an enthusiasm for jazz which remained with him throughout his life.

In 1940, Larkin went up to St John's College, Oxford, to study English in the expectation of being called up for war-service after a year; he failed his army medical exam and graduated in 1943. Oxford influenced him a great deal, not only because of the people he encountered there but because of its war-time atmosphere. The uncertainties of the war, its austerities and restrictions and the depleted number of students meant that Oxford was a less youthfully high-spirited environment than usual. Since the future was so unpredictable, career aspirations seemed immaterial. Larkin commented of this period 'At an age when self-importance would have been normal, events cut us ruthlessly down to size'. This consciousness of limited horizons, of down-to-earth realism, is constantly present in Larkin's writings.

Larkin continued to write poems in Oxford, but never very rapidly and with only occasional publication. The first burst of creativity came after he left Oxford to take up a post as librarian in Wellington, Shropshire – a matter of chance rather than decision, for Larkin was obliged by the Ministry of Labour to take up the first job he was offered. The fact that Larkin remained a university librarian all his life (in Leicester, Belfast and Hull) thus represents a consequence of accident, and in his poems Larkin frequently comments on the tyranny of chance in our lives.

It was in 1944 that Larkin was invited to submit a collection to a publisher and he sent in thirty poems which appeared as *The North Ship* in July 1945. He also completed two novels, *Jill* and *A Girl in Winter*, both of which can very profitably be read in conjunction with his poems. For a time, Larkin was intent on writing more fiction and he only returned to consistent poetry-writing when he moved to Belfast in 1950. His work, occasionally published in journals, went largely unnoticed and his only major publication was a privately printed collection entitled *XX Poems*. When five of his poems appeared in a collection from the Oxford-based Fantasy Press he tried to distribute it to the leading literary critics, an effort jeopardised by his ignorance of the fact that postage charges had just been increased.

The breakthrough came in 1955 after Larkin had moved to Hull and found a responsive publisher in George Hartley of the Marvell Press, then based in Yorkshire. *The Less Deceived* was an immediate success and quickly established Larkin's reputation as a leading poet in Britain. Subsequently, Larkin's output was slow but widely acclaimed: *The Whitsun Weddings* was published in 1964 and was followed a decade later by *High Windows*. He also edited the prestigious and influential *Oxford Book of Twentieth Century Verse* published in 1973. Honours duly followed: he received the Queen's Gold Medal for Poetry in 1965 and the CBE in 1975. After the death of John Betjeman in 1984, Larkin was widely expected to succeed him as Poet Laureate, but the prospect did not appeal to him ('I wake up screaming', he wrote to his friend Kingsley Amis). Larkin fastidiously shunned publicity and towards the end of his life he wrote less and less poetry, not because he deliberately abandoned poetry but rather, as he wryly commented, because 'poetry left me'. Although it was Ted Hughes who succeeded Betjeman, Larkin has remained in the popular imagination as England's unofficial Poet Laureate. As well as the early novels, he published two further books of prose: *All What Jazz?*, a collection of jazz reviews and *Required Writing*, a collection of book reviews and miscellaneous pieces. He died on 2 December 1985.

Larkin's success in the mid-1950s coincided with the emergence of a group of poets dubbed the 'Movement'; the dullness of the title was seized upon by its critics as indicative of the dullness of the poems. Whether or not there was ever a consciously organised 'school' of poets is conjectural, but the publication in 1956 of an anthology entitled *New Lines* is now generally seen as marking a decisive moment in modern poetry. Larkin was included amongst the contributors and perhaps more than any of them has been taken to represent the essential characteristics of the Movement. Whatever unity the group had (a good number of 'Movement' poets have since denied any conscious association) began in a number of friendships struck up in Oxford and Cambridge in the 1940s. Herein lay a particular feature of the Movement, for its academic origins are everywhere evident: of the nine poets to appear in *New Lines*, six were university teachers. The poetry of the Movement valued intelligence as a prerequisite for creativity and this can be seen in the careful, probing thoughtfulness of Larkin's poems.

Critics in the mid-1950s were aware of a shift in taste evident in the work of Larkin, Kingsley Amis, John Wain, Thom Gunn, Donald Davie and others of the generation born in the 1920s. In 1953, Stephen Spender (one of the leading 1930s poets) had claimed that England was experiencing 'a rebellion of the Lower Middle Brows' and a year later Anthony Hartley amplified this. He found in the work of these writers a similar tone: 'cool, scientific and analytical. . . distrustful of too much richness or too much fanaticism, austere and sceptical. . . Complication of thought, austerity of tone, colloquialism and the avoidance of rhetoric – these provide some common ground and common dangers'. It was felt that the Movement writers were generally reacting *against* something, even if they did not appear to have a common aim in view. Most of the poets assembled by Robert Conquest in the *New Lines* anthology came from a lower-middle-class background in the North and Midlands. They represented an emerging intelligentsia in England whose origins lay not in the Establishment but in provincial grammar schools with sights set firmly on academic success. Faced with the bleak austerity of England in the 1950s, they reacted on the one hand to the social Utopianism of the 1930s poets which they had seen overwhelmed by the rise of fascism and totalitarianism and on the other hand to the neo-Romantic excesses of the leading 1940s poet, Dylan Thomas, who died of alcoholic poisoning in 1953. More than social realism or metaphorical richness, the Movement poets sought the directness of rational meaning and a prosaic familiarity of expression. The defensive asides and cautious qualifications which dominated the poems in *New*

Lines were attempts to appear careful, reasonable and modestly unassuming. Suspicious of idealistic systems and philosophies, these poets put their trust in rational structure and comprehensible language. They were concerned not to express bardic inspiration so much as common-sense reason.

Larkin's early reputation, then, was bound up with the critical response to the Movement of which he was a part and which is now accepted as a significant fact of our literary history. In that sense, the Movement succeeded in creating a period of conservatism in poetry, a period of retrenchment. Even as it succeeded, though, there were warning voices. The poet Charles Tomlinson, himself of the same generation as the Movement, launched an attack as early as 1957. He argued that the Movement poets were disablingly timid in their parade of ordinariness and modesty and that their aspirations were too limited. A few years later Donald Davie, one of the more adventurous of the Movement poets, was agreeing with him, censuring himself and the group as a whole for their 'pusillanimity' in their attitude to their readers. He argued that Movement poetry was insufficiently ambitious, that it did not demand enough either of the poet or the reader, that poetry in the hands of the Movement was too deferential to the expectations of the reader.

> We were deprecating, ingratiating. What we all shared to begin with was a hatred for writing considered as self-expression; but all we put in its place was writing as self-adjustment, a getting on the right terms with our reader (that is, with our society), a hitting on the right tone and attitude towards him.
> ('Remembering the Movement', *Prospect* (Summer 1959) pp. 13-16.)

By the 1960s, with a growing prosperity in Britain, the values of the Movement were further undermined by an era of social change and radical experimentation and soon the Movement receded as a period, according to its critics, of gloomy dullness. The Movement poets themselves developed more individual reputations; even by 1963, when Robert Conquest assembled *New Lines II*, Donald Davie was suggesting 'Divergent Lines' as a more appropriate title. But with or without the Movement, Philip Larkin's reputation has remained intact and enhanced since the mid-1950s. At a time when poetry was becoming more and more the possession of the expert and the academic, Larkin remained faithful to a fundamental principle: 'But at bottom poetry, like all art, is inextricably bound up with giving pleasure, and if a poet loses his pleasure-seeking audience he has lost the only audience worth having'.

2 THEMES

2.1 THIS ENGLAND

Probably more accurately than any other post-war poet, Philip Larkin has caught in his poems the authentic feeling and flavour of contemporary England. In *The Less Deceived* and *The Whitsun Weddings* he captures the England of the 1950s and 1960s with its post-war urban renewal, the expansion of suburban housing, its industrial ugliness and crowded city-centres all experienced alongside the tranquil backwaters of rural solitude. His poem 'The Whitsun Weddings' gathers together the open spaciousness of the Lincolnshire countryside, agricultural farmland, polluted canals, scrap-metal yards, a cooling tower and an Odeon cinema. Elsewhere, we find in 'Here' the bustling impersonality of a city-centre and its 'residents from raw estates'; the municipal parks and playgrounds of 'Toads Revisited' and 'Afternoons' with its 'estateful of washing'; the 'dark towns' which 'heap on the horizon' in 'Talking in Bed' and the 'fumes/And furnace-glares of Sheffield' in 'Dockery and Son'. One feature of contemporary urban England of which Larkin makes particular use is the multiplicity of advertising hoardings which ubiquitously parade images of a better life and which in 'Essential Beauty' swamp the surrounding bleakness. But there is also a more peaceful, beneficent rural England celebrated in 'At Grass', 'Here' and 'MCMXIV'.

More remarkable is Larkin's ability to convey the quality of ordinary life in the mid-twentieth-century. His poems reflect the way most of us live: dourly enduring the dreary routines of existence, gnawingly dissatisfied, prey to tantalising dreams and ideals beyond our grasp and occasionally surprised by happiness. 'Wedding-Wind', 'Coming' and 'Born Yesterday' (in *The Less Deceived*) show the possibility of contentment; 'The Whitsun Weddings' and 'An Arundel Tomb' are examples of Larkin at his most optimistic, even if that optimism is qualified. But for the most part, his poems portray life as meagre, disappointing, depleted. The subject of 'Mr Bleaney' is a man whose life is symbolised by his bare and cramped room. The speaker of 'Toads' fails to shake off the burden of routine. In

'I Remember, I Remember' the poet bitterly recalls the boredom of child-hood; in 'Dockery and Son' a middle-aged bachelor watches life pass him by. Larkin's urban settings show us the commercialised materialism of supermarkets where crowds 'Push through plate-glass swing doors to their desires' ('Here') or find themselves duped by the 'synthetic' and 'nature-less' fantasy-world of 'The Large Cool Store'. In 'Ambulances' disasters occur during 'Loud noons of cities' and are attended by 'children strewn on steps or road' and women rushing 'Past smells of different dinners'. Our urban life is characterised by impersonality, tedium, drabness and occasion-ally fear.

To be contrasted with this, though, are moments of pastoral content-ment. 'Here' presents a journey whose end is 'unfenced existence' and where 'Loneliness clarifies' our purpose and destiny. For Larkin, the value of the pastoral lies in its isolation. Away from the pressures of urban crowds and suburban uniformity, the individual can in seclusion confront his deepest instincts. As he reaches a more remote countryside, the speaker in 'Here' becomes aware not only of silence, but of a multitudinous life teeming around him of which he can be only barely conscious: 'Here leaves unnoticed thicken,/Hidden weeds flower, neglected waters quicken . . .' Moreover, he is assailed not just by what is present, but by the past em-bodied in the landscape, the generations of past inhabitants who populate the 'Luminously-peopled air'. This sort of perception is also to be found in the concluding poem of *The Whitsun Weddings*. As the poet ponders the significance of the memorial in 'An Arundel Tomb' he mentally traces the passage of history: 'Snow fell, undated. Light/Each summer thronged the glass. A bright/Litter of birdcalls strewed the same/Bone-riddled ground. And up the paths/The endless altered people came.' In soli-tude, in the silence of the countryside or cathedral, the individual is able to recover a perspective which reaches back into time and makes a context for the present. The slower, cyclical rhythms of the countryside restore us to ourselves, reminding us that we are the subjects of time. In 'MCMXIV' Larkin refers to 'the countryside not caring'. That is why it is so important to him. In building and rebuilding our towns, we foolishly believe ourselves to be masters of our environment and our destinies. In the countryside, we face the chastening indifference of a world bodied against us and beyond our control. Larkin celebrates the pastoral because it chastens our vanity.

2.2 THE INDIVIDUAL AND SOCIETY

Just as the settings of Larkin's poems are familiar, so the people in them have a concrete realism. With a keen eye for the telling detail, Larkin can set vividly before us the presence of particularised individuals who are also representative of a type. The character of Mr Bleaney is created by the drabness of the room he left behind and also by his routines: his preference for sauce to gravy, summer holidays in Frinton, Christmas at his sister's in

Stoke, all suggest his imprisonment in familiar habit. Similarly, the wedding-parties in 'The Whitsun Weddings' are characterised by an identifying detail. Fathers wear 'broad belts' and have 'seamy foreheads'; the uncle is caught 'shouting smut'; girls say their farewells whilst 'gripping their hand-bags tighter'. It is the pen of a novelist (Larkin wrote two novels in the 1940s) which is able to summon up a whole character in a few significant details. But Larkin's characters all serve to represent a type. His interest is not in their individualism so much as in their typicality. In Larkin's view, the notion of the individual as something unique is yet another of our illusions, for in reality our distinctiveness is blurred by the need to con-form within society and by the pressures society imposes on us.

Most of Larkin's poems show the individual trapped in circumstances beyond control. In 'Deceptions', a young woman suffers alone, alienated from the world outside which remains indifferent and hostile. 'Afternoons' depicts young mothers who are made identical with each other by their shared routines: 'An estateful of washing,/And the albums, lettered/*Our Wedding*, lying/Near the television . . .' They are subject to remote forces: 'Something is pushing them/To the side of their own lives.' Elsewhere, the individual is absorbed in an impersonal crowd, whether it be the dancers 'Shifting intently, face to flushed face' in 'Reasons for Attendance' or the 'residents from raw estates' who throng the town centre in 'Here', 'brought down/The dead straight miles by stealing flat-faced trolleys'. Individuality becomes submerged in impersonality: 'Broadcast' shows the concentrated effort in singling out a particular person (identified only by a dropped glove lying by outmoded shoes) from the 'Giant whispering and coughing' of a crowd. Hence the individual's yearning to escape, to be free not only of crowds, but of identity itself. The horses in 'At Grass' achieve anony-mity; 'Here' ends with a vision of vacancy; 'Wants' insists that 'Beneath it all, desire of oblivion runs'.

The individual is inevitably swamped by the mass; he is also caught up in its dreams and desires. Larkin's crowds in 'Here' and 'The Large Cool Store' surge towards the temporary gratification of materialist desires. In an age of relative prosperity (particularly the 1960s) the individual in Larkin's poems can prove his own self-worth only by a compulsive acquis-itiveness: 'Cheap suits, red kitchen-ware, sharp shoes'. We are rendered identical by the democracy of materialism. Moreover, our common fanta-sies are revealed to us by a familiar feature of our daily lives. In its adver-tising images, society represents to the individual its collective ideals and dreams. Both 'Sunny Prestatyn' and 'Essential Beauty' use the images created by advertisers to reveal our ubiquitous yearnings for perfection and happiness. In doing so, these advertisements show us not only the ideals pursued by society, but how far short of these ideals the individual is condemned to fall. In 'Faith Healing', though, Larkin shows how at a deeper level individuals are identical, sharing a fundamental nature: 'In everyone there sleeps/A sense of life lived according to love'. Indeed, the movement of Larkin's poems is frequently away from the particular towards the general in an effort to identify our common natures, our common plight, our common humanity.

2.3 RELATIONSHIPS

If the individual is out of place in society, Larkin's poems frequently show the individual doomed to failure in personal relationships. From first to last in these two collections, we find Larkin turning again and again to the futility and fragility of individual relationships between the sexes. The opening poem of *The Less Deceived* presents the speaker mourning over the photographs of a woman whose future belongs with someone else; 'An Arundel Tomb', the poem which concludes *The Whitsun Weddings*, explores the significance of a sculpture which has a knight and his lady holding hands.

'Reasons for Attendance' shows the poet as an outsider, eager for 'The wonderful feel of girls' but already sceptical of the notion that 'happiness is found by couples'. In 'Dry-point', Larkin explores one cause of dissatisfaction in our relationships. Our erotic natures imprison us; we are condemned to suffer the 'time-honoured irritant' of carnal desire which drives us on but always leaves us disappointed, the 'magic all discredited'. What we can never enjoy is the purity of a relationship unsullied by physical desire. Once married, Larkin's couples are usually trapped by each other in roles and routines. Arnold, in 'Self's the Man', 'married a woman to stop her getting away/Now she's there all day' and Arnold is pestered by 'nippers to wheel round the houses' and all the burdensome trivia of domestic duty. Larkin argues that there is no essential difference between Arnold, the busy family man, and himself, the middle-aged bachelor: 'He still did it for his own sake,/Playing his own game./So he and I are the same' because each chose their condition. However, in 'Dockery and Son' we see a more radical scepticism which not only doubts the efficacy of relationships and kinship but doubts even our power to choose. For 'To have no son, no wife. . . still seemed quite natural' to the speaker and although Dockery is a husband and father they are united in having lived according to 'what something hidden from us chose'. In forming our relationships, we are subject to the uncontrollable caprices of chance, accident and coincidence and upon these flimsy foundations do we build a shared life. Recognising this, it is no wonder that the protagonist of 'Wild Oats' is accused of being 'too selfish, withdrawn,/And easily bored to love'.

Since it is so difficult to know the truth about our own natures, to know another person intimately is beyond us. This is the subject of 'Talking in Bed', a poem which depicts the listless dissatisfaction of a couple lying together in bed. 'An emblem of two people being honest', in reality they have nothing to say to one another and are absorbed in themselves and the wind outside, not in each other. Beyond their relationship, 'None of this cares for us', but neither is there an explanation for their indifference to each other. What each of them does know is that it becomes more difficult not just to find words which are true and kind (as if they might be irreconcilable) but 'not untrue and not unkind'. The poem's final line suggests our predisposition for falsehood and selfishness. If it is our nature to be solitary, deceived and deceiving, then our relationships are doomed to failure.

Two poems in particular, though, take a more optimistic view of the possibility of finding happiness in relationships. The speaker in 'The Whitsun Weddings' is at first aloofly disparaging about the wedding-parties he sees but is finally drawn to a recognition of 'the power/That being changed can give' and the poem's closing images are redolent of fertility and fruition. And although 'An Arundel Tomb' suggests that 'What will survive of us is love' is only 'almost true', it does at least seem nearer to truth than to falsehood.

Relationships in Larkin's poems, then, are beset by difficulties and an inherent bias towards failure. Like so many other objects of our aspiration, love is an ideal which condemns us to disappointment. Although we have a notion of love, it seems remote from the reality which we actually experience and so in this sense is an illusion: it exists as an ideal for which we strive but which we cannot possess. In his poem dedicated to the jazz saxophonist, 'For Sidney Bechet', Larkin writes: 'On me your voice falls as they say love should,/Like an enormous yes'. But for the most part his poems show our failure in love. The widow in 'Love Songs in Age' mournfully recognises how 'that much-mentioned brilliance, love' which promised 'to solve, and satisfy,/And set unchangeably in order' failed to do so in her marriage 'and could not now'. The women in 'Faith Healing' are maimed not by physical ailments but by their lovelessness: 'That nothing cures'. They weep now because for a moment they believe that they have found the embodiment of love in the preacher even as they recognise its illusoriness, for 'time has disproved' it over and over again.

2.4 ILLUSION AND REALITY

Love is one of the perpetual illusions to which we are prey and as a poet Larkin repeatedly turns a disillusioned gaze onto reality and exposes its deceptions. The title of *The Less Deceived* shows us Larkin's usual poetic identity: watchful, guarded, not to be taken in, not born yesterday. In 'Born Yesterday', dedicated to the birth of his friend Kingsley Amis's daughter, Larkin wishes for her an ordinariness which, because it confers 'Nothing uncustomary/To pull you off your balance' will help her be 'dull', for only a 'skilled,/Vigilant, flexible,/Unemphasised' wariness can help her in the 'Catching of happiness'. The intended title poem of *The Less Deceived*, 'Deceptions', suggests that the raped girl is 'less deceived' than her victimiser because he laboured under the greater deception that the fulfilment of his desires was ever possible. She at least knows the

exactness of suffering, but he is condemned always 'To burst into fulfil-
ment's desolate attic', for we are constantly seduced by illusions, only to
suffer an angry disappointment. 'A Study of Reading Habits' - the scholar-
liness of the title is mocked by what follows - recreates the world of boy-
hood fiction and adolescent fantasy. But now the speaker does not read
much: 'the dude/Who lets the girl down before/The hero arrives, the chap/
Who's yellow and keeps the store,/Seem far too familiar. Get stewed:/
Books are a load of crap'. These figures are familiar not only from the con-
ventions of a particular literature, but because the poet now recognises
that life is full of failures, not heroes; familiar, too, because the poet
recognises himself in them.

Time offers illusions. Memory idealises and glamourises the past; antici-
pation leads us to expect too much of the future. 'Next, Please' symbolises
the future as a ship which, though 'Arching our way', never anchors: 'it's/
No sooner present than it turns to past'. The future suddenly turns itself
into a fleeting present before receding from us into the past, a past over
which we cast a haze of nostalgia. Childhood, for example, is recalled by
Larkin as 'a forgotten boredom' ('Coming') or else, in 'Take One Home for
the Kiddies', an age of greed and careless cruelty. In 'I Remember, I
Remember', Larkin mocks the clichés associated with childhood in order
to deflate our habitual nostalgia. 'Triple Time' considers the relationship
between past, present and future in a more abstract way. The present is
empty and colourless, 'A time unrecommended by event'. But this present
was once eagerly anticipated as the future, 'An air lambent with adult
enterprise', something fulfilling and purposeful. And this same present will
one day be retrospectively recalled as the past, nostalgically summoned up
as full of 'fat neglected chances/That we insensately forbore to fleece'. The
present will be looked back on as a past of missed opportunities, chances
which went begging. But we live only in a continuous present which in
itself has no purpose or meaning except as they are falsely imposed from
the perspective of the past or the future. Time itself brings only 'seasonal
decrease', an inevitable decline towards death.

'Reference Back' states that 'though our element is time,/We are not
suited to the long perspectives/Open at each instant of our lives'. Time
holds us in its thrall. It teaches us not to expect too much of the future,
nor to think too well of the past, but it is a lesson we never seem to learn.
The substance of time is the endless process of generation, decay and re-
generation which denies uniqueness and seems purposeless. The young
mothers in 'Afternoons' are conditioned and determined by a force which
'is pushing them/To the side of their own lives' just as the speaker in
'Dockery and Son' is mastered by 'what something hidden from us chose'.
In 'Send No Money', the speaker is taught the lesson of 'the way things
go': *'Sit here, and watch the hail/Of occurrence clobber life out/To a
shape no one sees . . .'*. That 'hail of occurrence' is delivered by time and
we are robbed of any power even over our own lives. Our illusions are a
way of evading this uncomfortable truth. Time and experience should

teach us the fraudulence of our self-deceptions for in being less deceived we will not be happy, but we may be less unhappy.

2.5 TIME

How, then are we to salvage any sense of purpose and meaning in life? Some poems suggest the possibility of happiness: 'Wedding-Wind', 'Coming' 'For Sidney Bechet', 'Broadcast', 'The Whitsun Weddings'. Other poems argue their way to a more positive conclusion. 'Church Going', for example, moves from scepticism to affirmation in the speaker's discovery of a 'hunger in himself to be more serious'. In an age without religious faith, the church is simply the object of superstition. But because it has been for so long associated with our most deeply moving moments in life – birth, marriage and death – it signifies our need to ritualise and memorialise. It is 'proper to grow wise in' because, as the 'suburb scrub' around it deteriorates further, it acts as the symbol of our deepest desire: a need to preserve. The paradox of time is that it both erodes and preserves. The stone monument in 'An Arundel Tomb' has preserved an 'attitude' which 'Time has transfigured . . . into/Untruth'. Time has preserved not the Latin inscription, but the clasped hands of husband and wife. Even if only 'almost true', the emblem of their love has nevertheless endured.

A number of Larkin's poems show a desire to escape time, to escape even the self in order to experience an ultimate truth. 'Wants' and 'Absences' in *The Less Deceived* celebrate conditions of vacancy. In *The Whitsun Weddings*, the same impulse is present in 'Here', 'Water' and the title poem. All end with a vision of release and fulfilment symbolised in elemental images of sky, sun, water and rain. Larkin is not 'religious' in the orthodox sense, but he is deeply responsive to symbols which represent for him permanence and endurance, stillness and tranquillity.

3 TECHNICAL FEATURES

3.1 RHYME, RHYTHM AND SYNTAX

The stylistic features of Larkin's poetry show his use of traditional resources which are frequently modified and varied. His poems are usually stanzaic – that is, they are composed of stanza units of a regular length. However, to avoid the monotony of repeating identical structures, Larkin uses various techniques to overcome the rigidity of the stanzaic form. Almost invariably, for example, his stanzas run on from one to another so that the formal stanza divisions are blurred by a surging continuity. This tension between formal regularity and freedom is fundamental to Larkin's stylistic achievements.

Larkin uses rhyme in different ways to secure different effects. In 'Next, Please' we find simple couplets ('we/expectancy', 'day/say', 'clear/near', 'waste/haste', etc.) whilst in 'I Remember, I Remember' a highly complex rhyme-scheme is used. Sometimes, Larkin uses a simple rhyme-scheme to portray simple-mindedness as in the speaker's naivety in 'Next, Please'. The regular alternate rhymes (a/b/a/b) of 'Mr Bleaney' help to convey the monotonous routine of his life whilst in 'Naturally the Foundation will Bear Your Expenses' the nursery-rhyme-like simplicity helps us to perceive the shallowness of the academic jet-setter. However, a more complex rhyme-scheme, combined with larger stanza units, generally reflects a complex development of thought in a poem. This can be seen, for example, in 'Church Going', 'The Whitsun Weddings' and 'Here'. An examination of the pattern of rhymes in 'Faith Healing' shows a typical intricacy: the ten-line stanzas follow an ornate repetition of a/b/c/a/b/d/a/b/c/d. This network of interlinkings is an unobtrusive principle of organisation and unity by which the seemingly casual, extempory play of thought is given a logical inevitability. Moreover, in the final stanza we find a significant departure from the scheme in the half-rhyme between 'loved/disproved' so that the poem ends on a jarring note literally and metaphorically.

In some poems, Larkin makes greater use of half-rhyme (sometimes known as slant-rhyme or para-rhyme) whereby a rhyme repeats consonants but the vowels are not full-rhymes (as in 'work/weak'). 'Reasons for Attendance' shows a mixture of half-rhymes ('share/sheer') and full-rhymes ('here/sheer') so that the consistently full-rhymes of the final stanza mimic the speaker's sense of hollow security. Similarly, the half-rhymes of 'Toads' help to create the speaker's lack of assurance. In 'Toads Revisited', we find a similar use of half-rhyme (note the inventiveness of 'failures/lobelias'!) with an occasional full-rhyme at moments of conviction: 'Not a bad place to be./Yet it doesn't suit me' and at the poem's conclusion: 'Give me your arm, old toad;/Help me down Cemetery Road'. In 'Afternoons', Larkin uses no rhyme-scheme at all, thereby helping to suggest the drifting aimlessness of the mothers' lives. But the absence of rhyme is hardly noticeable because of Larkin's use of partial assonance (the resemblance of sound between vowels, for example, 'fading . . . fall in . . . bordering') and alliteration (the repetition of an opening letter in a sequence of words, as in 'At swing and sandpit/Setting free their children'). This gives the poem a musical flow, a sonorous gravity appropriate to its sombre conclusion.

Larkin's rhythms show the same tension between regularity and freedom, between metrical organisation and the freedom of spoken language. His basic measure is the iambic foot (a light stress followed by a heavy stress) often repeated five times in a line (hence, iambic pentameter) and this is traditionally the metre which in English most nearly approximates to the conversational flow of the speaking voice. This is the metre most frequently used by Larkin: 'Lines on a Young Lady's Photograph Album', 'Maiden Name', 'Wires', 'Church Going', 'I Remember, I Remember', 'Faith Healing' and 'The Whitsun Weddings' all show Larkin's control of the iambic pentameter. ('At Grass' and 'An Arundel Tomb', two poems possessing interesting resemblances, resemble each other too in using an iambic tetrameter, that is, four iambs to the line.) Of course, not every line in these poems is a perfect iambic pentameter. Many lines do fall perfectly into the pattern: 'Its five light sounds no longer mean your face' ('Maiden Name'); 'It pleases me to stand in silence here' ('Church Going'); 'Or how their lives would all contain this hour' ('The Whitsun Weddings') but unvaried repetition soon creates monotony. Within any one line, then, Larkin will introduce metrical variations to disrupt the iambic pattern without destroying it, or to keep the formal rhythm unobtrusive (as in 'Deceptions' or – a more extreme example showing deliberate rhythmical looseness – 'Wedding-Wind'). Larkin's achievement is thus to capture the inflexions, pace and movement of a speaking voice. So, for example, in 'Church Going' the iambic pentameter renders both the casual colloquialisms of the first stanza (where the iambic measure is frequently varied) and the stately gravity of the final stanza, where the metre is much more strictly sustained.

Larkin's control of syntax also creates variety and freedom within controlled structures. In 'Toads', the syntactical unit (sentences or clauses) is contained within the stanzaic divisions so that the poem feels to have a step-by-step progression. But usually Larkin drapes lengthy syntactical structures over the framework of lines and stanzas. His sentences swing over line-endings, often to stop in the middle of a line; similarly, they take no account of stanza divisions but surge from one to another. Within this loose, flowing movement, Larkin can create sudden and significant contrasts. The first sentence of 'Here' travels through twenty-four lines before suddenly pulling up; it is then followed by a series of parallel sentences each beginning 'Here'. The syntax creates an effect of stillness at the end of a long journey. Larkin's syntax also conveys the experience of thinking, of ideas being taken up or dismissed, developed and concluded. Look how the syntax of this extract from 'Dockery and Son' tracks a developing idea with its false starts, hesitations and abrupt conclusions:

> Dockery, now:
> Only nineteen, he must have taken stock
> Of what he wanted, and been capable
> Of . . . No, that's not the difference: rather, how
>
> Convinced he was he should be added to!
> Why did he think adding meant increase?
> To me it was dilution . . .

3.2 IMAGERY

A superficial impression of Larkin's poetry might suggest that it is relatively bare of imagery. Because it is so rooted in the phenomena of our everyday lives, it seems to be full of concrete *things* - cooling towers, advertising hoardings, the random items which Larkin assembles into lists in 'Church Going', 'Here' and 'The Whitsun Weddings'. But a closer look at the poems shows how frequently if unobtrusively Larkin exploits the capacity of language to render feelings and impressions vividly and completely. Broadly speaking, images are comparisons: what is asserted is a similarity or identity between things and by comparing things in this way the poet is able to communicate to us his particular idea or state of feeling. A comparison which is made explicit, usually by the use of the words 'like' or 'as' ('He's as brave as a lion') is a simile; when the comparison is implicit ('We must iron out the problem') so that 'like' or 'as' is not used, we have a metaphor.

Let us begin by investigating some simple similes in order to see their effects. In 'Deceptions', Larkin describes the shame and suffering of a young woman after a sexual violation: 'All the unhurried day/Your mind lay open like a drawer of knives'. The knives, of course, suggest sharpness, as if her pain is literally lacerating. But her mind is 'open like a drawer', exposed, out in the open when it should be enclosed, and what this simile suggests is not just the 'sharpness' of her pain but also her feeling of exposure, as if nothing now can be private. In 'Ambulances', we find the ambulances surprisingly compared with 'confessionals'. This at first gives us the impression of cloistered silence, but confessionals are also places where the sinner unburdens himself secretly and so the ambulances are made to assume not only an intense privacy and solitariness but also a strange kind of relief. Larkin's similes are notable for their startling accuracy; they are not far-fetched yet always seem just and inevitable even if they are more expressive than they first appear. For example, in 'At Grass' the poet asks rhetorically of the horses: 'Do memories plague their ears like flies?'. Who would have thought that memories are like flies? Yet this seems absolutely right: they hover around our heads, often annoyingly, they are distracting and stubbornly refuse to be dispersed. What Larkin suggests here is that we succumb to memories like a disease (in the metaphor of 'plague') and he manages to make the abstract notion of 'memories' vividly concrete and tangible in the simile with 'flies', which are themselves literally present around the horses' heads.

His metaphors are likewise resonant and particular. 'Deceptions' opens with the concrete apprehension of the woman's grief: it is a 'taste. . . Bitter and sharp with stalks, he made you gulp'. Her grief is firstly associated with the taste of the drug she is forced to drink, but her grief is also 'sharp', as sharp as the stalks (of straw, perhaps) on which she was forced to lie. Again, the abstract notion of 'grief' is given tangible force and concreteness. Larkin controls his metaphors so well that we easily pass over them. In 'Church Going' he identifies the abiding importance of churches as marking the place where 'all our compulsions meet,/Are recognised, and robed as destinies'. 'Robed' perfectly suggests the church rituals and ceremonies by which our most significant moments in life are celebrated and memorialised. More startling still is Larkin's ability to convey exalted emotional states with astonishing simplicity and accuracy. In 'For Sidney Bechet', love is described as 'an enormous yes' and in 'Faith Healing' 'a crowd/Of huge unheard answers jam and rejoice' when the women believe themselves finally to have discovered love. Language as direct as this is a language made exact.

Larkin's poetry not only names the things familiar to us in our everyday world. It also endows phenomena with a symbolic resonance. At a simple level, a toad becomes a symbol of work: it squats oppressively, it 'soils/With its sickening poison' and 'Its hunkers are heavy as hard luck'. Similarly, in 'Next, Please' the future is symbolised as a 'Sparkling armada of promises' in which only one ship (of death) seeks us, 'a black-/Sailed unfamiliar'. But Larkin often uses more complex symbols. In 'Dry-Point' he envisages an ideal state of being unsullied by our sexual instincts as 'that bare and sunscrubbed room,/Intensely far, that padlocked cube of light', where it is the associations of sun and light which suggest purity. These symbols occur quite often in Larkin's poetry. 'Here' ends with the poet 'Facing the sun' at the shore's edge, and 'Water' uses the traditional elemental symbols of water and light. 'The Whitsun Weddings' concludes with the procreative image of rain to suggest how the couples' futures lie before them waiting to burst into life. It is often the case that as the speakers of the poems become more reflective and ratiocinative during the course of the poem, they have increasing recourse to the language not of abstract thought but of concrete imagery and symbolism.

3.3 TONE AND DICTION

When reading a poem, you should be aware of the tone of voice in which it might be spoken. Just as in normal speech your tone varies from the flippant and familiar through to the earnest and serious, so in poems you should sense the writer striking and often adjusting the tone of voice. This is particularly true of Larkin's poems, for he has made himself the master of tonal variations, controlling the language so that it suggests a particular tone of voice. How, then, is the poetry to indicate an appropriate tone? This is a complex matter, involving the poem's meaning, its rhythms and structure. But diction plays a large part: that is, the different levels of language from which the poet selects his vocabulary. So, the diction we use in everyday conversation represents a language that is idiomatic, familiar, colloquial; at other times a more elevated, formal language is more appropriate. The directness of Larkin's poems, our impression of an individual personality speaking to us, comes from the kind of diction he uses and the tone of voice that it establishes.

Some of his poems achieve their effects by a variation of tone and diction. 'Church Going' begins on a note of casual ease with the colloquial language of conversation: 'some brass and stuff/Up at the holy end' creates for us a speaker who is slightly bored, uninformed and incurious. But by the end of the poem, the diction is more formal and elevated, suggesting how the speaker's attitude has shifted from scepticism to absorbed thoughtfulness. Similarly, 'Dockery and Son' moves from the extemporary language of anecdote ('Was he that withdrawn/High-collared public-schoolboy') to a diction more scrupulous and probing: 'They're more a style/Our lives bring with them: habit for a while,/Suddenly they harden into all we've got'. This movement from the colloquial to the elevated is quite common in Larkin's poems, representing the way in which their speakers are gradually absorbed in an unexpected train of thought which began with a triviality they were inclined to dismiss.

Sometimes, the bluff, no-nonsense tone of his poems comes from the sudden eruption of slang or coarse diction. 'A Study of Reading Habits' (note the mock-academic title) ends angrily: 'Get stewed:/Books are a load of crap.' Similarly, the angry frustration with which Titch Thomas punctures illusion in 'Sunny Prestatyn' is conveyed by the uncompromising language describing his defacement of the poster. Other poems sustain a diction which, because it is more dignified, suggests a tone of stately. gravity. 'At Grass' develops the elegance of the horses by way of the elegance of its own language (the wind 'distresses' tail and mane). 'An Arundel Tomb' strikes a note of sublimity by using a language that is formal, decorous, almost ceremonious. But the keynote of Larkin's poems, the standard from which he departs, is the diction of intelligent conversation, the language of a poetic personality that is rational, reasonable and not easily deceived.

3.4 IRONY AND SATIRE

Irony is an almost constant presence in Larkin's poetry. This is inevitable, given his major preoccupation with the disparity between illusion and reality. The structure of experience is itself ironic: appearances are exposed as false, expectations are disappointed, deceptions are painfully revealed. Irony is a technique by which a statement is made to carry an import which is the opposite of, or suggests something very different from, what is literally said. It is a technique we use frequently, usually for the purpose of mockery. The word 'irony' itself is a Greek word, meaning something like 'dissimulation', a pretence. Larkin's poems are often built on this framework of irony, whereby a self-deception is exposed as the falsehood it really is. So, for example, the rapist in 'Deceptions' is caught up in the illusion that fulfilment is possible through the satisfaction of carnal appetite. Ironically, he is the greater victim than the girl he rapes: she is 'less deceived, out on that bed,/Than he was, stumbling up the breathless stair/To burst into fulfilment's desolate attic'. Similarly, the putative adventurer in 'Poetry of Departures', 'Stubbly with goodness', has failed to escape his fundamental illusion that life can be made perfect. Irony of a more obvious kind is evident in 'Sunny Prestatyn' and 'Essential Beauty'. The poster of the inviting girl in the first of these poems is defaced because 'She was too good for this life'; she is destroyed not because we disapprove of the poster, but because, ironically, we desire her image all too fiercely. Similarly, in 'Essential Beauty' there is a mocking irony in the representation of the 'Well-balanced families' who owe their contentment to 'that small cube each hand/Stretches towards'. The tone of voice tells us that this is palpable nonsense we are invited to believe.

Another technique, closely allied to irony, by which Larkin alerts us to our illusions, is satire. Satire is a principle of exaggeration by which our follies and vices are held up to ridicule; it is both comic in caricaturing features of human behaviour and moral in its aim of social improvement. In Larkin's poems, it operates in a particular way, through the use of the clichés associated with our popular illusions and self-deceptions. For example, the meaning of 'A Study of Reading Habits' emerges entirely through the conjunction of clichés and their final, abrupt deflation. Those clichés are deliberately inflated, for the point of the poem is that we recognise them as clichés. The language is that of juvenile fiction, stuffed with dreams of 'keep[ing] cool', dealing out blows to 'dirty dogs', imagining 'ripping times' in the dark. In the world of adolescent clichés, sex is a brute weapon, women yielding and succulent 'like meringues'. By the end of the poem, the speaker is disenchanted with these illusions and the clichés are now the clichés of failure and far from helping him to escape dull reality they merely remind him of what is 'too familiar'. In 'Poetry of Departures', Larkin satirically exploits the clichés of fiction. The cavalier defiance of *'He walked out on the whole crowd'* is made equivalent to the stereotyped conventionality of *'Then she undid her dress*/Or *Take that you bastard'*, thereby suggesting its fatuous falsehood. In 'I Remember, I Remember', Larkin's satire goes a stage further. He mocks the inflated language of juvenile romance whilst at the same time negating it: 'And here we have that splendid family/I never ran to when I got depressed,/ The boys all biceps and the girls all chest... I'll show you, come to that,/ The bracken where I never trembling sat,/Determined to go through with it'. The comic inflation of the clichés is thus punctured by the insistent negatives and by their own conventionality. This use of a negated cliché is found elsewhere in the poem; the speaker has returned to 'where my childhood was unspent' and concludes that ' "Nothing, like something, happens anywhere" ' where the quotation marks remind us of the cliché that is here inverted. Indeed, this technique is to be found in other satirical poems. Wild oats were never sown by Larkin in the poem of that title and he keeps photographs of the girl he failed to court as 'Unlucky charms' to remind him of his failure. Given his attitude to reality, it seems natural that Larkin should express himself through negatives: if 'Life is slow dying' then 'it leaves/Nothing to be said' ('Nothing To Be Said').

3.5 DRAMATIC MONOLOGUE

We are constantly aware in reading Larkin's poems of an individual presence speaking to us directly. We are addressed by a recognisable voice which reveals to us a particular sort of character who shares with us his thoughts and feelings. The majority of the poems are written in the first person so that we are directly confronted with the shifts and turns, inflexions and nuances of a whole personality. It is dangerous to assume that the character speaking these poems is always Philip Larkin himself. Rather, Larkin creates different sorts of characters (personae) in his poems, almost as an actor assumes masks to play different parts. Hence, in the discussions of the poems that follow I have frequently referred to 'the speaker' of the poem or 'the voice' or simply 'the poet', rather than attribute every thought and feeling to Larkin himself. In this sense, the poems are monologues uttered by a character who reveals something of himself to us.

How does Larkin convince us of the identity of the speaking voice? Much depends on its *naturalness*, so that we easily identify with a voice that sounds familiar. The tone is affable and inviting, anecdotal in relating situations and experiences which are ordinary and commonplace: a train journey, a visit to a church or supermarket, watching mothers and children in a park. The language is conversational, often using slang and idiomatic phrases, rooting us in an everyday world of familiar objects. Reflections are prompted by trivial incidents: discovering old song-books; looking through a photograph album; watching new-born lambs. The poems deal with familiar emotions: nostalgia, regret, disappointment, loneliness, occasionally even happiness. And the voice tracks, with sinuous fidelity, the twists and turns of thought, the shifting of emotions. In its hesitations and qualifications, assertions and retractions, it sounds thoroughly reasonable, urgent but careful in its sifting for the truth. We trust the voice because it sounds like our own; it is ourselves to whom we listen, our own hopes, doubts, fears, our own quizzing of life. In Larkin's poems we hear the voice of the common man in the mid-twentieth century: rational, tentative, not easily taken in but still enchanted by dreams, lonely but compassionate, querulous but wanting to be grateful.

So there emerges from Larkin's poems a consistent personality, one which insists on the necessity of honesty in looking at life squarely and unflinchingly. Romantic idealism is unerringly punctured: childhood is either 'a forgotten boredom' or else, in 'Take One Home for the Kiddies', a time of greedy insensitivity. Nature is hostile, a 'vast unwelcome' which portrays for us a mindless circularity of growth and decay and which in itself mocks man's transience. Relationships are fraught, belittled by our carnal instincts and then nullified by our essential isolation and selfishness. Religion is an illusory comfort, expressing our unanswerable bewilderment and disconsolation. The poems are the expressions of the speaker's honesty to the truth of his experience. And if the purpose of that honesty is to reveal purposelessness, what, you may ask, is the point of Larkin writing his poems at all? It is as if Larkin defends himself from the encroaching darkness by exposing it. His one act of supremacy is in the poetic activity itself, in shaping and ordering his experience through his mastery of language to produce a created artefact, what the American poet Robert Frost called 'a momentary stay against confusion'. Larkin's speaker makes his poems in order to preserve: to preserve his memories, thoughts and feelings, and thus to preserve himself.

If the speaker in Larkin's poems insists on an honest assessment of the world, he also insists on honest self-assessment. The speaker in 'Church Going' knows that he is 'Bored, uninformed' but also hunts down his reasons for visiting the church and discovers his own 'hunger in himself to be more serious'. In 'Mr Bleaney', the speaker is uncomfortably aware that in condemning Mr Bleaney he must condemn himself, just as in 'Dockery and Son' he is forced to recognise that his own life has been subject to incalculable and random accidents. But beyond his unsentimental acknowledgement of life's realities, the speaker is irresistibly drawn towards the ideals he wants to dismiss, particularly the ideal of love. Love may be likely to disappoint, but the speaker never condemns the urge to love. 'The Whitsun Weddings' presents a persona that is typical: sceptical, bored, a middle-aged bachelor who is aloofly observant of the newly-married couples. But by the end of the poem he has shared in a feeling of momentous change because of the affection and tender regard he gradually brings to the occasion. What redeems the personae of Larkin's poems is a sympathy and compassion which stubbornly survives the suffering of disillusionment.

As well as presenting us with a particular sort of character, Larkin's poems are often 'dramatic' in other ways. What is meant by this is that some of his poems enact little dramas in suggesting a particular situation that is developed. In 'Lines on a Young Lady's Photograph Album', for example, we are aware of the presence of a second party, the woman herself who 'at last' yields up the album and whom the poet mockingly rebukes: 'Not quite your class, I'd say, dear, on the whole'. Similarly, in 'Maiden Name', the married woman is addressed directly: 'Try whispering it slowly./No, it means you'. More commonly, though, Larkin develops the speaker's thoughts and attitudes in the poems by a process of internal dialogue: that is, the speaker reaches a conclusion by conducting a debate with himself. This technique is evident in 'Reasons for Attendance' where the speaker proceeds by a sequence of questions he addresses to himself: 'Why be out here?/But then, why be in there? Sex, yes, but what/Is sex?' The development of thought in 'Church Going' is made by way of self-questioning, a series of steps progressing towards a conclusion. The poems in *The Whitsun Weddings* make less use of this question-and-answer technique but nonetheless many show the same structure of an internal debate whereby the speaker rationalises with himself. The title-poem takes us through the stages of the poet's detachment, his gradual awareness of the wedding-parties, his aloof dismissiveness and then his quickening sense of involvement. The drama here is the drama of the mind's activity as it suddenly responds to a stimulus and launches out on a train of thought.

In some poems, Larkin uses the form of internal dialogue not to proceed to a rational conclusion but to expose the self-defensive twists and turns which hide beneath the appearance of rationality. In 'Mr Bleaney', the speaker condemns the room's previous occupant with a ferocity born of a lurking fear that he is actually stepping into Mr Bleaney's shoes. 'Self's the Man' similarly exposes the hollowness of the speaker's attempted self-justification. In comparing himself with his friend Arnold, who is burdened by his children, work and domestic routine, the poet seeks to show that in truth he is no less selfish than Arnold. The opening magnanimity of 'Oh, no one can deny/That Arnold is less selfish than I' is immediately undermined by the derisiveness of 'He married a woman to stop her getting away/Now she's there all day'. As the speaker describes Arnold's life of duty and responsibility, what we sense is not the speaker's admiration but his animosity and contempt for a man he actually regards as weak-willed and spineless. In the sixth stanza, the poet shifts his argument in order to assert that since Arthur 'was out for his own ends' and 'Playing his own game' in taking on marriage and fatherhood he is as motivated by self-gratification as the bachelor-poet. The only difference is that 'I'm a better hand/At knowing what I can stand' suggesting that the speaker is wiser than Arnold in knowing the limits of his tolerance. Having begun in praise of Arnold, what the speaker has revealed in the poem is a derisive, self-justifying superiority which attempts to hide the possibility that in fact the speaker is both more selfish and less happy than Arnold. The admission finally surfaces in the self-doubting last line: 'Or I suppose I can'. The drama of a poem like 'Self's the Man' is the drama of self-revelation, when a character suddenly becomes aware of a dismaying truth which, by the cosmetic appearance of logical argument, he has attempted to evade.

4 THE POEMS

4.1 THE LESS DECEIVED

Lines on a Young Lady's Photograph Album

This, the opening poem of *The Less Deceived*, contains a number of features typical of Larkin's poetry. There is first the creation of a speaking voice which makes us feel that the poet is addressing us directly. We find, too, a development of thought and attitude in the poem as ideas are taken up, modified and concluded. There is a characteristic movement from the particular to the general: from a specific situation (the poet browsing through a young woman's photograph album) there grows a general reflection on the significance of the experience. The tone of voice varies from idiomatic, off-the-cuff light-heartedness to a more serious and thoughtful exploration of meaning. So adept is Larkin's technical control that we barely notice the carefully balanced formal structure of the poem: the nine stanzas divided into three equal sections which mark the stages of the poem's development; the strict iambic pentameter and a/b/b/a/b rhyme-scheme; the emphasis which is made to fall naturally on crucial words and the witty punning.

The poem's opening immediately implies a dramatic situation – not, that is, a situation of tense excitement, but simply one in which the presence of another character is suggested. The speaker has, after some difficulty, persuaded the playfully reluctant woman to show him her photograph album: here is a familiar situation with which we can easily identify. Opening the album, the speaker does not know where to begin and his gaze is overwhelmed by so many pictures of the woman's past: words such as 'glossy', 'thick', 'confectionery', 'rich', 'choke', 'nutritious', 'hungers', wittily exaggerate the speaker's eagerness to consume as many pictures as possible. He begins to flick through the album before being taken aback by seeing the woman photographed with other men: the line 'Not quite your class, I'd say, dear, on the whole' suggests he is slightly hurt and wants to remind her that he is more suited to her than the 'chaps who loll/At ease' in her photographs (where we feel the faint disapproval behind the word 'loll').

The fourth stanza marks a shift in the poem's development as the speaker reflects on his reaction to seeing the woman's past contained in the photographs. He praises the art of photography as 'Faithful and disappointing': faithful because it candidly presents things as they really are; disappointing because we are thereby confronted with the blemishes in reality. This 'candour' (truth-telling) strengthens his feelings for the woman in the photographs because it presents him with 'a real girl in a real place' in a way that, say, a flattering portrait of her could not. In the fifth stanza his perspective changes: he is moved by the photographs because they represent a past which is irrecoverable and hence painful to recall.

> These misty parks and motors, lacerate
> Simply by being over; you
> Contract my heart by looking out of date.

Notice how the halting run-on 'you/Contract' gives the words extra weight so that we sense how his feelings for the woman are intensifying, particularly when we recognise the pun on 'Contract', suggesting how he is pained by the remoteness of the woman's past and simultaneously drawn closer to her ('Contract' in the sense of engaged, bound).

The final three stanzas bring his reflections to a conclusion. Moved and pained by feelings of poignant nostalgia, the speaker decides that these feelings are due to an exclusion from the woman's past which leaves him free to yearn for that past precisely because he is uninvolved in it and has no responsibility for it: 'We know *what was*/Won't call on us to justify/ Our grief'. He is 'left/To mourn' her past as an outsider and the snapshots which have frozen brief moments in her life 'condense,/In short, a past that no one now can share' even though her future might belong to someone other than him. Finally, he is grateful for the photographs because they preserve her in her past where she lies 'Unvariably lovely' (that is, that loveliness is unalterably preserved by the photographs). If that image of her becomes 'smaller' as we recede in time from it, it is also 'clearer', framed and memorialised by these photographs.

From the apparently simple business of looking through a woman's album, the poem moves into a touching reflection on memory and time, and the importance of memory in preserving the past even though recollection of it causes some pain. Returning to the title, we might notice a pun: the 'Lines' are the poem but also the lines of age which will befall both the poet and the woman; but age cannot wither the past moments preserved by the photographs. Hence, the photographs are cut free from the ordinary transitoriness of life; like memory itself, they are painful because they preserve what is irrecoverable.

Wedding-Wind

'Wedding-Wind' is deliberately placed after 'Lines on a Young Lady's Photograph Album' to serve as a stylistic contrast. The strict formality and anecdotal detail of 'Lines' gives way to a more relaxed structure (a loose five-stress line and occasional rhyming) and a more imagistic, heightened style which tries to capture an intensity of feeling.

The poem describes a woman's feelings on the first days of marriage and how the constant high wind comes to be associated with her almost mystical joy. We are immediately presented with that unignorable, insistent wind and the opening lines show an emphasis on the sounds of words: the repeated 'w' of 'wind. . .blew. . .wedding'; the assonance of 'night' and 'high'; the repetition of 'again and again' create a sense of fluidity which is reinforced by the repeated conjunction 'And', together with the present participles 'banging', 'leaving', 'hearing', 'seeing'. This flowing movement imitates the constant surge of the wind which dominates the woman's thoughts and her sense of fulfilment is experienced in the closing full rhymes of 'back. . .sad. . .lack. . .had'.

The following day, the woman is aware only of the wind: 'All's ravelled under the sun. . . All is the wind/Hunting through clouds and forests'. Now she comes to identify her own joy with the activity of the wind, as if the joy which runs through all her actions ('like a thread/Carrying beads') is embodied in the wind itself with a strength that is almost unbearable. Like the morning's wind, her love is so intense that the 'morning' of her love (it 'shares my bed') seems 'perpetual'. In a further sequence of images drawn from nature, she wonders whether even death can end ('dry up') her love ('new delighted lakes': the suggestion is of endless abundance). The final image, of cattle kneeling to drink water, beautifully captures her feelings of gratitude and blessedness expressed in the religious connotations of 'kneeling' and the plenitude of 'all-generous waters'. The 'waters' symbolise love as inexhaustibly offering the source of all life. By the end of the poem we are persuaded that nature itself in the presence of the wind shares in and manifests the woman's joy. There is an essential unity between herself and the natural world which makes her love not personal but a universal principle of life.

The poem shows Larkin working in a different vein from 'Lines on a Young Lady's Photograph Album', able to create a depth of feeling in the emotions of a newly-married woman and allowing his meaning to grow suggestively out of images rather than directly stating it. Although the poem seems to portray the woman's exultant joy, there is also a lurking sense of threat. The woman is for a time alone on her wedding-night when her husband has to shut the door blown by the wind and she is left 'Stupid in candlelight. . ./Seeing my face ·in the twisted candlestick,/Yet seeing nothing'. The image is slightly macabre and conveys something sinister about her sudden loneliness. This confused mixture of feelings is also felt in her being 'sad/That any man or beast that night should lack/The happiness I had'. Later, the wind is 'hunting' and 'thrashing' dangerously, and the suggestions of boundless love at the end of the poem are in fact expressed as rhetorical questions. What Larkin captures in this poem are the ambiguous feelings of a woman on her wedding-night: her joy, but also her fears and vulnerability.

Reasons for Attendance

In this poem Larkin attempts to explain why he commits himself to the isolated life of the artist in preference to the ordinary fellowship of everyday life. As he passes a dance-hall (rather less exotic places in the 1950s than now!) he hears the music and watches the young couples dancing 'on the beat of happiness'. He imagines what it would be like to be one of them and is momentarily excited by the prospect of 'The wonderful feel of girls'. He recognises that what attracts the dancers inside is a sexual urge which seeks a partner for fulfilment but he also decides that happiness is not to be found entirely in partnership. By contrast, he is drawn another way, towards an individual fulfilment in art. It is the individuality of art which draws the poet rather than the merged communality of the dance-hall. His art is a calling (hence the image of a bell sounding) which can be experienced only in an individual way; if the tolling bell represents the search for happiness it can only be heard by different people in different ways. Happiness is not to be found by any one single means, and believing this the poet is content, or so he persuades himself, to remain outside, excluded from the dancers who seek happiness in their own, different way. So it seems a conclusion is found, until we reach the sting in the tail of the poem: 'both are satisfied,/If no one has misjudged himself. Or lied'.

The ending of the poem strikes a note of doubt which echoes back through the whole: how easy it is to persuade ourselves that what we want to believe is true. In a final recognition, the poet suspects himself of glib self-justification, of implausibly convincing himself that he can find happiness in solitariness. The poem is interesting in creating a tone of voice which we can easily hear, and which ends up suspecting itself. Is the poet right to suspect himself of lying?

If we look closely at the poem, we may find that behind the apparent confidence of the speaking voice there lurks a self-doubt. We might begin by noting how the young dancers are described: their faces are 'flushed', they are 'shifting intently' and 'Solemnly', almost as if stupefied by 'the smoke and sweat': later, they 'maul to and fro'. This is an unflattering portrait, perhaps excessively so: from the start, the speaker does not want to envisage what he sees as too appealing a contrast to his own loneliness. Then we watch the to-and-fro of his internal debate: 'Why be out here?/ But then, why be in there? Sex, yes, but what/Is sex?' which in its balance has all the appearance of reasonableness. But then the debate lapses into prejudice: 'Surely' is a rhetorical device, seeking unthinking assent and the dash in the second stanza's final line is a dismissive and hectic dash towards a desired conclusion: 'sheer/Inaccuracy, as far as I'm concerned'. The colloquial asides ('But then', 'yes', 'Surely', 'as far as I'm concerned') which look like the shifts and hesitations of reasonableness are in fact evasive because the poet is anxious to justify his own point of view and reach a conclusion on which he has already decided. The individuality he thinks is celebrated in art may in fact be an imprisoning loneliness. There is a deliberately rigid parallelism in the final stanza: 'Therefore I stay out-side,/Believing this; and they maul to and fro,/Believing that' which sounds like a properly balanced conclusion. But the argument is deliberately weighted in favour of the speaker and it is a poet's honesty which ends the poem darkly, 'Or lied'. Fundamentally, he is not convinced by the argu-ment in favour of individuality which might in truth simply mean solitary isolation. He is more envious of the dancers than he cares to admit. The poem's honesty comes about because of the lurking self-criticism which is ultimately acknowledged and made explicit in the poem's final words.

Dry-Point

'Dry-Point' follows 'Reasons for Attendance' as a companion-piece, even perhaps as a corrective. If the previous poem wilfully undervalued the need for sexual fulfilment, 'Dry-Point' explores our sexual instincts much more honestly, although the conclusion it reaches is hardly less gloomy.

Sexual urges are seen as an endlessly repetitious 'irritant', for as soon as they are satisfied they begin their demands once more. Sexual instinct is a 'bubble' which silently inflates and traps us, making us creatures of our erotic natures. The only way to overcome its demands is to satisfy them animalistically: 'Bestial, intent, real'. In an explicit image of sexual con-summation, Larkin describes how the sexual 'bubble' is burst: 'The wet spark comes, the bright blown walls collapse'. But to burst a bubble is, colloquially, to shatter an illusion, and the third stanza describes the barren unfulfilment which follows the promise of sexual satisfaction: 'hills' are 'ashen', the lakes 'shrunken'. There is no 'magic' in sex; like a golden ring which turns out to be lead, the experience of sex discredits it ('Birmingham magic' refers to the place where cheap imitation rings made of lead were manufactured). Trapped by an illusion of fulfilment which leads only to disappointment, Larkin summons up images of austere purity from which our sexual natures exclude us: a 'bare and sunscrubbed room,/ Intensely far, that padlocked cube of light' which we can only imagine, never experience, and into which our sexual instinct can 'obtain no right of entry'.

Clearly, human nature is flawed for Larkin because we are prey to our own appetites, imprisoned by our own desires. He might be criticised for taking a bleak view of our sexuality, but Larkin uses it to show how the structure of human nature which eagerly anticipates happiness and fulfil-ment, in fact condemns us to disappointment. The same theme is to be found more explicitly in 'Next, Please', which reminds us that only one expectation can be fulfilled, only one ship (in whose wake 'No waters breed or break') will come in – death itself.

Wants

'Wants' is an important poem because it reveals an attitude which lies at the heart of much of Larkin's poetry. In 'Reasons for Attendance' and 'Dry-Point' we have seen how he rejects the idea that happiness is to be found in the communality of ordinary social and sexual life. 'Wants' comes as a logical conclusion in proposing that our natural condition is of isolation and that, given the disappointment and suffering inherent in existence, what we most yearn for is non-existence.

The poem captures a sense of weariness, felt in the sluggish iambic pentameter of the two refrains ('Beyond all this, the wish to be alone', and 'Beneath it all, desire of oblivion runs') with their heavy mid-line caesuras (pauses), and in the structural parallelism of the two stanzas. Each is a single sentence opening and closing with the same line and a three-line 'list' coming in between. The effect is of exhaustion and monotony as the sentence toils through the intervening lines to a repetition of its opening – lines which are themselves metrically more clumsy than the refrain. In those two refrains, we find a weary vagueness, a curt dismissiveness: 'Beyond all this', 'Beneath it all' suggest how life both confines us (we want to go 'beyond') and weighs heavily on us (we have to dig 'beneath' it). The first stanza declares our need for solitariness in the face of oppressive and cramping social demands: invitation-cards obscure the sky threateningly; sexual activity is routinely mechanical (following 'printed directions') and family loyalty is a matter of tribal convention ('the flagstaff' suggests a spurious unity). The second stanza proposes that far from trying to escape death, we fundamentally yearn for our own annihilation. However much we plan for the future or seem to ward off death (taking out life insurance as protection, having children to carry on the family line, refusing to contemplate death) what we actually want is 'oblivion'.

The poem suggests that a desire for anything other than solitariness and death is an illusion. The images of communality in the first stanza are all hollow; similarly, the second stanza implies that by turning away from the inevitability of death we turn towards illusion. Expectations in the future can only be disappointed: the 'tensions of the calendar' are 'artful', deceptively raising and then dashing our hopes. The phrase 'life insurance' is a lie because nothing in life (except death) can be guaranteed; 'tabled fertility rites', like 'the printed directions of sex', sounds aridly mechanical and even ignorantly pagan; we avert our eyes from death at some cost because we pay for it in our illusions.

If 'Wants' is a bleak poem, it is nevertheless an attempt by Larkin to express what he sees as the truth about existence. The abruptness of the title sounds clamouring, demanding; the poem surprises by its steady gravity and the simplicity of its 'wants'. If we find other poems by Larkin (such as 'Wedding-Wind') much more celebratory of life, Larkin is not so much contradicting himself as expressing different moods, one in which he is responsive to the beauty of life, another in which he exposes the truth of his vision of it.

Maiden Name

'Maiden Name' is characteristic of Larkin in exploring a generally-experienced situation. The poem is addressed to a recently-married woman and asks what significance her maiden name holds now that she has acquired her husband's surname.

In the opening stanza, the poet (perhaps teasingly) proposes that in changing her name the woman has lost identity with all the associations of her maiden name; she cannot be the same as she was before. Discarded, her maiden name belongs to the past, only to be found among the trivia of her girlhood and adolescence. Since it belongs irrevocably to the past the poet wonders what meaning her maiden name can now have: in what sense can it be 'true' of her now? As the second stanza runs into the third, the poet begins to define an answer. Since her maiden name encapsulates the woman's past, the associations it still carries mean 'what we feel now about you then': her beauty, intimacy, youth are captured in her former name. The recollection of her maiden name vividly brings to mind all that she once was, so that her old name 'shelters our faithfulness', representing all the affection and longing the poet felt and still feels for her. By the end of the poem, the poet has discovered that far from losing its significance the woman's maiden name has assumed greater meaning in embodying all his feelings for her now that she is lost to him.

But before we build a romantic plot of thwarted love around the poem, we must note that the poet writes not from a first-person 'I' point of view but a more general 'we'. Perhaps this is a distancing technique, a way of reducing the speaker's personal involvement. On the other hand, there are moments of waspish irony in the poem which suggest a barely-controlled jealousy. For example, what are we to make of the fourth line's 'thankfully confused'? This seems a dutiful gesture of politeness to the new husband, but is undermined by the final stanza when the poet nostalgically recalls 'Those first few days' when the woman was 'unfingermarked'. This last word has a contemptuousness about it which makes the husband a cheapening molester of the woman. And the final line seems to refer to her married name, and therefore the husband, as 'depreciating luggage', a burden of little value which the woman must now bear.

All this contributes to the complex variations of tone in the poem. The development of the poem moves through three stages, each marked by the opening line of the three stanzas. It is as if the slightly puzzled, possibly light-hearted attitude to the woman of the opening stanza (look what you've given up now that you're married!) gradually deepens into an emotional compliment to her. The crucial shift comes precisely half-way through the poem. Until then, the language is mostly simple and concrete, the lines usually neatly end-stopped, the tone sprightly and clever. But at the dash mid-way through stanza two, it is as if the poet suddenly surprises himself at the seriousness of his question: 'Then is it scentless, weightless, strengthless, wholly/Untruthful?' That seemingly clumsy run-on line suggests a perplexed pause as the speaker searches for the right word: what 'truth' does the woman's maiden name have? We are made aware of the directness of a speaking voice, the dramatic situation of two interacting characters when the speaker asks 'Try whispering it slowly./No, it means you' where we imagine the woman speaking her former name at the line break. And then there is the developing thought, the modification of attitude as the speaker feels his way towards an answer to his question: 'Or, since you're past and gone,/It means what we feel now about you then' with the hesitation on 'Or' as a new idea is taken up, and its metrical stress on the crucial words 'now' and 'then'. The movement of the verse perfectly captures a speaking voice and the shifting emotional pressure behind it: 'How beautiful you were, and near, and young', reveals in its heavy pauses a voice trying to find the right (and simple) words, a voice surprised by and even wary of its emotional intensity. Perhaps that is why the speaker shelters behind 'we' rather than 'I'. The lightly-tripping iambic ease of 'Marrying left your maiden name disused' deepens throughout the poem into a more complex and personal feeling. The mood is one of nostalgic regret for something lost, something that time has taken away, and this mood is common to many of Larkin's poems.

Church Going

One of the best known of Larkin's poems, 'Church Going' shows masterly technical control and develops a typical Larkinesque persona and attitude. Once again, the poem begins with a specific and familiar experience before pondering its general significance; the conversational, anecdotal quality deepens into an attitude and language more thoughful and reflective.

The speaker, not quite knowing why, stops to visit an empty church, browses around, embarrasses himself by reading too loudly from the lectern and leaves somewhat uncomfortably reflecting that 'the place was not worth stopping for'. The poem then traces a line of thought which develops from this incident: having no knowledge of or interest in churches, why does he always feel drawn to visit them? Since most people are as bored by them as he is, churches will inevitably be abandoned: what will happen to them then? Perhaps a few cathedrals will be retained 'chroni-cally' as items of historical interest; the rest will fall to ruin and become objects of superstition. But then, like belief, superstition itself must die and only a crumbling edifice will remain, its purpose lost in history.

As he imagines this church falling into disuse, then, he wonders who will be its final visitor: someone with an esoteric interest in church archi-tecture, perhaps; or an enthusiast of ruins, or someone sentimentally trying to summon up the ceremoniousness of a church-service. More appropriate than all these would be someone like the speaker who, under no illusions about the church containing any residue ('silt') of the divine, nevertheless makes his way there deliberately because it preserved for so long the rites associated with three fundamental moments in life: birth, marriage and death. Unable to evaluate the significance of the church, he yet knows that 'It pleases me to stand in silence here'. Amidst the endless flux and trivia of life, the church stands as a monument to all that is most 'serious' and enduring. Because it houses the most crucial moments of our lives, the church has a stabilising and harmonising ('blent') influence in reminding us that the choices we make in life and our conduct of it are not to be taken lightly. This particular function of the church, at least, can never be obsolete, 'Since someone will forever be surprising/A hunger in himself to be more serious'. In representing this 'seriousness', the church, or whatever physically remains of it, will always be the proper place 'to grow wise in' if only because the presence of so many dead is a sobering testament to life's fleeting transitoriness.

Within the poem, Larkin manages to create a vivid portrait of the character of the speaker. 'Bored' and 'uninformed', he stops to visit the church almost unwillingly. His attitude at the beginning is one of flippant scepticism. He checks that no service is taking place (he does not want any of that!) before entering; here is just 'Another church' with its familiar accoutrements over which the eye roams uninterestedly and we are told offhandedly about 'some brass and stuff/Up at the holy end' ('stuff' and 'holy end' revealing the speaker's bored ignorance). What strikes him most is the silence, 'tense, musty, unignorable' out of which he makes a tedious joke: 'Brewed God knows how long' (God presumably does know). Clumsily dutiful, he removes his cycle-clips as a sign of respect. At something of a loss to know what to do, the poet stares at the roof for interest, but his ignorance ('Cleaned, or restored? Someone would know: I don't') cuts him short. So he does what everybody is tempted to do in an empty church: mounts the lectern, reads out loud and is startled by the echoes which 'snigger briefly'. The word 'snigger' does a lot of work here, for it is not the echoes which 'snigger' but the speaker's attitude which is sniggering. Like a nervous schoolboy, his attitude is actually one of uneasy scepticism and cultivated disdain: he pretends an indifference he does not really feel, evidenced by his conventional if 'awkward' reverence and his embarrassment at hearing his own voice. His dismissive reflection that it was not worth stopping to visit the church is insecure. It has disturbed him more than he cares to admit and he is forced to fathom out his true motives for stopping, to discover that the place means more to him than he was at first prepared to concede. We feel the presence of a man speaking to us and to himself easily and naturally, carefully exploring and explaining his experience, shifting from conversational flippancy to earnest musing.

Our sense of a particular personality emerges from Larkin's control of his language, a language which allows modern colloquialisms ('some brass and stuff', 'God knows') to coexist easily with more elevated vocabulary such as 'accoutred' and archaicisms like 'blent'. We start off in the idiom of familiar conversation and easy anecdotal style, as if launching out on a story, 'Once I am sure there's nothing going on. . .', until the sentence is concluded with the emphatic weight of the repeated vowel in 'thud shut', given two thudding stresses by the speaking rhythm which imitate the bang of a closing door. Now we are inside the church, and the listing of 'matting, seats, and stone,/And little books' has the cinematic quality of a roving camera. Notice how this lengthy second sentence is segmented into short phrases (marked by the semi-colons) as the eye takes in details indiscriminately. This inconsequentiality continues until we reach the deliberate *gravitas* of 'I peruse a few/Hectoring large-scale verses', where the pomposity of 'peruse' and 'Hectoring', by contrast with the preceding everyday diction, mimics the rhetorical grandeur of the verses which he reads aloud. The incident is closed at the end of the second stanza with an end-stopped line whose finality is clinched by its regular iambic metre.

As the poet defines his experience more scrupulously, the diction begins to shift towards a more thoughtful and resonant language. Having portrayed himself as ignorant about churches, the speaker nonetheless knows about 'parchment, plate and pyx' even though there is an obvious contemptuousness for 'one of the crew/That tap and jot' (felt in the derisive 'crew') and the 'ruin-bibber, randy for antique' (a bibber is one who imbibes alcohol, and what is thus implied is someone who has an inordinate enthusiasm for ruins). As he begins to define the attraction of the church, the language becomes richer. The poet's representative is to be found 'tending to this cross of ground' (churches are built in the shape of a cross), meaning that he is both drawn towards it and, in honouring it, takes due care of it ('tending'), particularly because he has had to make his way to it through 'suburb scrub', the dishevelled conditions of contemporary life. He begins to value the church because 'it held unspilt/So long and equably what since is found/Only in separation' (which prepares us for the later word 'blent') as if the church is a vessel for a precious liquid it keeps undisturbed. As the speaker (and his 'representative') finds himself 'gravitating' to the site of the church because of its 'seriousness', so we find the language gravitating towards a more abstract level and meditative tone. The clipped brevity of the phrases in the first stanza gradually expands into the assured, flowing rhythm of the final stanza as the poet reaches certainty.

So, on closer reading, the poem is far from being an expression of snide cynicism about the importance of churches as it seems to be at its opening. The 'church' may indeed be 'going' (the title contains a characteristic pun) but our need for it will survive. The church may represent an illusion: the music of the 'small neat organ' only obscures the more eloquent 'unignorable silence' of eternity and the superstitions which might succeed the church express a yearning in man for the transcendent and the mystical which the poet insists are illusory (simples do not cure a cancer). But the poet is neither as 'bored' nor as 'uninformed' as he pretends to be: he is thoughtful, probing, imaginative. He surprises himself by his hunger to be more serious, to find a permanent value in human life, to find that its incidental accidents and compulsions are in fact magnificently 'robed as destinies'. The poem ends with an affirmation of faith in man's integrity and a refusal to drift into a cynicism that depreciates human life.

Toads

One of Larkin's best-known poems 'Toads' is popular for its expression of the constricting weariness of work and the apparent attractions of carefree liberation from routine.

The first two stanzas develop the odious burden that comes with the necessary routine of work. It is a 'toad' which squats oppressively on life and which, if the poet were clever enough, he could escape. It is a loathsome blight on life which it 'soils/With its sickening poison'. The imagery conveys a mixture of disgust and anger but its comic exaggeration suggests that this is an explosive outburst of somebody releasing pent-up feelings knowing that they are not entirely reasonable. The following three stanzas continue with this tone of exasperation: 'Lots of folk live on their wits. . . Lots of folk live up lanes' – so why not him? He pictures the hand-to-mouth, freebooting life-style of those who have thrown off work and yet manage to survive: 'They don't end as paupers. . .They seem to like it. . . No one actually *starves*'. These are the people he should envy, but his envy is only superficial, for what is discernible in these stanzas is a deeper tone of disparagement. This is felt first in the excessive alliteration of 'Lecturers, lispers/Losels, loblolly-men, louts' where we feel the speaker groping to justify his assertion that 'Lots of folk live on their wits' and finding himself at a loss to identify them, lurching through a random list held together only by alliteration. The portrait of the folk who 'live up lanes' in the fourth stanza is frankly unappealing and although 'They seem to like it' the speaker sounds unconvinced. The fifth stanza makes more explicit his underlying distaste, with its offhand reference to 'nippers' and the contempt for 'unspeakable wives. . . skinny as whippets'. The speaker tries to envy them but he fails to disguise his disapproval; at bottom, his endurance of the daily grind in fact gives him a moral superiority.

The sixth stanza marks a shift in tone as the speaker draws to a recognition of his true condition. He admits to a lack of courage 'To shout *Stuff your pension!*', knowing that for him it is a fantasy, the stuff of dreams. For he has absorbed too completely the work-ethic and now the 'toad' is part of his nature, leaving him free only to hanker after the fruits of success: 'The fame and the girl and the money'. But there is once more a suggestion of disapproval here, for these are the clichéd images of pulp-fiction won by those who 'blarney', who deceive others and perhaps themselves into thinking that such success is possible or even desirable 'All at one sitting'. Again, what is proposed as an object of envy is in fact qualified by a fundamental disapproval. Only if we catch this note of self-criticism can the suddenly-complex final stanza fall into place, for by the end of the poem, the speaker has come to realise that working and not working are not alternatives but complementary. Whichever way you choose, you will always desire the way you rejected, either because of its freedom or its security. To choose one way entails not commitment but only the suspension of choice, for the alternative is always available. To work or not to work is neither more nor less admirable than its alternative. But for the poet, 'It's hard to lose either/When you have both', because his discontent with the daily grind of work leaves him free to enjoy the prospect of rebelling whilst enjoying the security of work. This honest self-appraisal which ends in an admission of complacency (he knows he will not give up work but can thereby enjoy the temptation of doing so) reconciles the two sides of his personality in a grudging acceptance of habit and routine.

The poem's form is that of a debate which brings together conflicting desires and impulses in an effort to arrive at the truth about the poet's nature. It shows a rationality which refuses to take things at face value and which strips away layers of illusion with self-critical honesty, and this is one of the hallmarks of Larkin's poetry.

Poetry of Departures

Like 'Toads', 'Poetry of Departures' explores our capacity for self-delusion. It takes up the same subject, that of choosing between a life of adventurous freedom or ordered dullness. Once again, we find that both life-styles are criticised as they are in 'Toads'.

We need to note how at the outset of the poem news of the man who 'chucked up everything' comes 'fifth-hand', as a remote and unprovable rumour. We are expected to approve of him, but the ironic hyperbole of 'audacious, purifying,/Elemental' gives away the poet's lurking suspicion. He admits that 'We all hate home' and the punctiliousness of a life arranged 'in perfect order'. We are thrilled by the prospect of abandoning it all, but that thrill is only akin to the juvenile escapism which responds to '*Then she undid her dress*/Or *Take that you bastard*'. Nevertheless, the possibility of escape from his monotonous routine keeps the speaker 'Sober and industrious'. Then the argument takes a sudden turn which involves two wonderfully comic images of daring escape: to 'swagger the nut-strewn roads' portrays the arrogance of one who trusts to luck; 'Crouch in the fo'c'sle/Stubbly with goodness' wittily associates the self-satisfaction of 'goodness' with the man who lets himself go (exemplified by his not shaving). Both these images belong to a childish imagination and so they contain an implied criticism of their 'hero' figures which Larkin identifies as their 'artificial' quality:

> Such a deliberate step backwards
> To create an object:
> Books; china; a life
> Reprehensibly perfect.

The man who cavalierly throws everything up and 'lives on his wits' (as 'Toads' puts it) is caught in the very same illusion as the speaker who keeps 'The good books, the good bed,/And my life, in perfect order': both believe that a perfect life is possible. Both lives are artificial, evasive, a deliberate step backwards from the truth that life is always dissatisfying and to act otherwise is 'reprehensible'. There is no 'poetry' (romance, escape) in 'departures', except in our idealistic and illusory view.

Triple Time

We have seen that a number of poems in *The Less Deceived* are dominated by a sense of time's inexorable passage bringing disillusionment and disappointment. 'Next, Please' shows us 'Always too eager for the future', excitedly awaiting the 'Sparkling armada of promises' which draws in so slowly until suddenly it is 'No sooner present than it turns to past'. It is as if we spend our lives not in the present, but in a state of anticipation of the future which suddenly becomes a past, leaving us painfully disappointed by the things that did not happen. The present is a ghostly, ephemeral transition between expectation and disappointment.

This is the theme of 'Triple Time', the title suggesting the division of time into past, present and future (marked by the three stanzas) as well as a rapid musical tempo (how quickly time flies!). The division is false, for the 'present' only exists in relation to other time (its past and future); like 'a reflection', it is itself empty. Just as the street is empty, the sky bland, the air 'a little indistinct', so the present moment is boringly 'unrecommended by event'. And yet this present moment was once eagerly anticipated in childhood which invested the future with the excitement of 'contending bells' rather than the dullness of the 'empty street' and 'sky to blandness scoured' which constitute the present. The line about 'An air lambent with adult enterprise' beautifully captures the child's excited expectation of his future's fulfilment in the lovely serenity of 'lambent' (a gentle radiance) and firm purposefulness of 'enterprise'.

The present exists in another relationship too, as a past which will be remembered with regret. As the object of nostalgia it will also be seen as something other than it really is: 'A valley cropped by fat neglected chances/That we insensately forbore to fleece'. The image suggests that in the past we failed to notice the rich and fertile opportunities surrounding us. But this is an illusion which the future makes of the past, for the present moment is irredeemably 'empty'. Nevertheless, we need this illusion of missed opportunities to constitute 'our last/Threadbare perspectives' so that as we grow old ('seasonal decrease') we can blame the past for our current misfortunes rather than confront the truth of the matter. The present is created either by past anticipation and imagination or by future memory: in itself it is nothing. Hence, we can only live in an almost constant alteration of illusion and disillusionment as hope turns to disappointment.

Deceptions

Originally entitled 'The Less Deceived', this poem is in effect the title-poem of the collection. It is written as a response to a passage from Henry Mayhew's book *London Labour and the London Poor* in which a young woman describes how she was drugged and raped. (Henry Mayhew's book, first published in 1861–2, is a record of his investigations into the life and work of the poor and underprivileged of Victorian London.) Larkin's poem summons up the girl's shame and isolation before exploring further the significance of the incident and deciding that the rapist was as much a victim as the girl he raped.

The poem begins with Larkin identifying himself with the girl and pitying her. Even though it occurred long ago, the incident stands for Larkin as a portrait of cruelty. He can 'taste the grief' as she had to taste the drug the man made her gulp. The abstract 'grief' is made vividly particular in 'sharp with stalks', the stalks of the bed or floor on which she is forced to lie. Afterwards she has to live with her shame, a scar that will not heal. Larkin pictures her locked away in hiding, inconsolable, suffering the mortifications of dishonour. She is in darkness hearing only the 'Worry of wheels' outside (it is she who is 'worried', of course, not the wheels, but her tortured imagination makes the world take on her own condition). She feels an outcast, rejected by 'bridal London' (pure, virginal, unsullied) which 'bows the other way', unfeeling and unpitying. She feels exposed in an unremitting light which hunts her down and 'drives/Shame out of hiding'. Tormented, anguished, horrified, she finds time dragging by and she can feel only a savage pain: 'Your mind lay open like a drawer of knives'.

But the second stanza withdraws from this compassionate recreation of the girl's feelings to a more distant rationality as we return to the present: 'Slums, years, have buried you'. Compassion, after all, could not console her; indeed, it is almost an insult to assume that her suffering could be lessened by our pity. Instead, Larkin offers a generalised comment on her experience. 'Suffering is exact': in the girl's case, suffering is 'exacted' from her, she is aware of her own suffering and knows precisely its cause. But what of the rapist? In his case, where desire takes charge, 'readings will grow erratic': his suffering is more vague, an 'erratic' (and erotic?) misreading of man's true condition. For of the victimiser and victim, it is the victim who is the 'less deceived'. The victimiser is caught in the belief that his will can be fulfilled, a belief which the final image exposes as an illusion, for his fulfilment is in truth a 'desolate attic'. The girl is the less deceived because her suffering was imposed on her, not inherent in her, and she knows its cause; by contrast, the man is ignorant of the cause of his suffering ('stumbling up the breathless stair'), a victim of the universal illusion that desires can be gratified, wishes fulfilled.

The poem, then, passes a moral judgement on the experience it describes. Is Larkin right to feel that the victimiser is in fact the greater victim of his illusions? It is certainly a challenging view which makes the raped girl the lesser victim. Perhaps we might say that Larkin is not so much callous (about the girl) as moved to compassion for the plight of humanity emblematised by this incident: one suffers at the hands of another whose own suffering lies in a self-deception leading to an endless cycle of disillusionment.

The argument of the poem may be debatable, but the writing is admirable. The first sentence puts us into the scene with a piercing dramatic immediacy before the longer sentence explores the girl's feelings. Her sense of exposure and vulnerability is caught in the insistent, all-embracing light, 'unanswerable and tall and wide', when all she wants is darkness and oblivion; this diffusive image is followed by the clarity and sharpness of her mind being like an open drawer of knives. And the second stanza, although it shifts our sympathies towards the man, still recognises the woman's suffering: 'out on that bed' makes her isolated, cast adrift, with a suggestion of disgust for 'that bed'. The final image expresses with simple economy what the experience signifies. The man struggles exhaustedly 'To burst' upon the object of fulfilment but finds instead a 'desolate attic', a sudden emptiness in which he, like the forlorn girl, is also abandoned. As in 'Dry-Point', the attempt to satisfy our desires only reminds us of our true condition: lonely, disconsolate, doomed to dissatisfaction.

I Remember, I Remember

The title refers to a sentimentally nostalgic poem by Thomas Hood (1799–1845) which begins 'I remember, I remember,/The house where I was born,/The little window where the sun/Came peeping in at morn' and continues in similar vein. Larkin's poem challenges the romanticism of Hood's vision of childhood by proposing instead (like 'Triple Time') that our childhood is the creation of a glamourising memory which prefers not to recall reality as it was but to reconstitute it through a haze of nostalgia.

Travelling by train with a friend on an unfamiliar route, the speaker suddenly recognises the railway-station at which they have stopped as Coventry, his home town. Notice how the surprise of the discovery is caught by the syntax which has the exclamation 'Why, Coventry!' burst out before its natural place at the end of the sentence. In a flush of enthusiasm, he cranes out of a window for a recognisable sign but, comically, cannot locate himself at all. Deflated, he tries to summon up an appropriate nostalgia: 'From where those cycle-crates/Were standing, had we annually departed/For all those family hols?' but the train's departure cuts off his recollection. Thwarted and disappointed, he stares at his boots until his companion's question prompts a train of bitter reflections. The phrase 'have your roots' used by his friend is a cliché expressing a romantic attachment to his home town which the poet cannot in all honesty feel: 'No, only where my childhood was unspent', with its witty negative, expresses the uneventful emptiness of reality. Now he is able to define his childhood by its utter remoteness from the clichés popularly associated with it. Stereotyped images are summoned up in order to be discredited: he was not a child-prodigy, was not favoured by a conventionally lovable eccentric ('an old hat'), did not find shelter in the bosom of his family, was not surrounded by heroic brothers or beautiful sisters and did not discover a rural retreat (the phrase 'Really myself' stands exposed as an empty cliché). Neither did he experience the trembling intensity of a first love (again mocked by the cliché of 'all became a burning mist'), nor was he celebrated as a budding writer. Aware of his gloom, his friend interrupts him, prompting the poet to deliver the truth in that isolated, proverbial last line:' "Nothing, like something, happens anywhere".'

Characteristically, the poem is a progress towards clarification and honesty. The comic exaggeration and ironic use of stereotyped language mocks the romantic view of childhood which sees in it an idyllic happiness and innocence. The mounting bitterness contained in the satire expresses an anger that childhood, like all time that is present, is 'unspent'. But the anger is also directed at the speaker himself, and like so many others, this poem of self-appraisal is also an act of self-criticism. For the poet is angry at himself for having entertained romantic illusions about his past which have to be cruelly dashed; after all, ' "I suppose it's not the place's fault" '. This bitterness is actually exaggerated, and this can be seen in the catalogue of romantic illusions. The simple negative of 'did not invent' and 'wasn't spoken to' is repeated with ever-increasing emphasis. The irony is progressively sharper in 'here we have that splendid family' and 'I'll show you, come to that' before the accumulating anger is broken off by the companion's interruption, ' "You look as if you wished the place in Hell," ' which calms the poet into expressing his disillusionment in more subdued fashion. The poet's anger is caused not just by disappointment in his own childhood so much as by regret that it was nothing more than it was. Whilst rejecting the stock romantic clichés, he nevertheless wishes that childhood might be closer to what Hood's sentimental poem describes.

The language of the poem is prosaically conversational, a finely-tuned idiom in which all the nuances of feeling are caught. In particular, it shows up the preposterous conventionality of the clichés associated with childhood felt even in the phrase 'family hols', which seems to belong to a particular class in a bygone age. Against the background of colloquial, matter-of-fact tone and diction, phrases such as ' "have your roots" ', ' "Really myself" ' and ' "all became a burning mist" ' are, as their quotation marks in the poem testify, absurdly pretentious. Mockery is also present in the hyperbole of 'Blinding theologies', the pulp-fiction argot of 'she/Lay back', the far-fetched detail of the doggerel set in 'blunt ten-point' (a size of print). The diction appears bluntly ordinary, but in a very sophisticated way catches the shifting moods of a speaking voice.

The poem's rhyme-scheme is highly complex. Although the poem is divided into seven stanzas each of five lines and a final tail-line, its rhyming unit is actually one of nine lines so that the tail-line, so distinctively separated from the rest of the poem, is in fact integrated into the rhyming pattern. The nine-line rhyming unit is itself ornately symmetrical:

a b c c b a a b c/d e f f e d d e f/g h i i h g g h i/j k l l k j j k l

with rhymes in each unit revolving around two pairs of couplets. Apart from admiring the technical expertise involved in this, we ought also to ponder its effect. When overlaid on the stanza unit, the rhyming pattern is forever shifting, the rhymes occurring at different places within the stanzaic structure. This slightly puzzling displacement (we are vaguely aware of a regular rhyme-scheme on first reading but cannot quite place it) helps to create precisely that nagging familiarity felt by the poet before recognising his home town and the disorientation he feels when identifying what did not happen there: the rhymes, like 'nothing', seem indiscriminately to happen 'anywhere'.

At Grass

'At Grass' closes the collection on a note of gentle tranquillity, the mood of melancholic musing sustained by the careful diction, the slow progression of detail and reflection and the steady syntactical development.

The anonymity of the retired racehorses is established by the fact that they are referred to imprecisely as 'them' and at first are barely visible until the wind disturbs their tails and manes. The word 'distresses' is deliberately abstract and unenergetic, a slight archaism which keeps the tone of voice a little elevated above the colloquial and the mood calmly reflective. The next two stanzas recall their famous days as racehorses when they were fabled; though recollection is 'faint' and 'faded', their names have become part of a folk-memory of 'classic Junes'. The poet's imagination briefly recreates the scene of a race-meeting, the shorter phrases (marked by the colons) indicating a quickening excitement. The final, longer phrase ending stanza three beautifully creates a gradually sinking movement imitative of the 'long cry' of the race result which metaphorically hangs in the air before reaching the stop-press columns of the newspapers. The line-break at 'the long cry/Hanging' creates a moment of (literal) suspense which is continued through the repeated aspirates of 'Hanging unhushed'.

Stanza four returns us to the present scene with a highly effective simile: 'Do memories plague their ears like flies?' The simile makes the abstract notion of 'memories' firmly concrete whilst the verb 'plague' suggests how memories, like flies, are an unwelcome annoyance. The shake of the horses' heads to clear the flies seems to function as a response to Larkin's rhetorical question: they are disturbed by flies, but it is he who is disturbed by memories. For now that their time is past, they are content to stand in the 'unmolesting meadows', unmolesting, that is, because they are not 'plagued' by memories. Their identity inheres in their past fame ('Almanacked'); now they are anonymous, have escaped their identities ('slipped their names') and are 'at ease,/Or gallop for what must be joy.' They are alone, free of the field-glasses and stop-watch, visited only by 'the groom, and the groom's boy' in the evening of their lives.

The poem takes up Larkin's familiar themes of identity, time and memory, but in this poem he finds a peacefulness, a contentment in these horses that he cannot find in himself or in human life. In his memory, he recalls the time fifteen years ago when the racehorses were famous: the race-meetings, the 'Squadrons of empty cars' (arranged in straight lines of military exactness), the 'heat' which contrasts with the 'cold shade' in which they now shelter. Now, in their retirement, the horses have retreated from their former world and can gallop for no other motive than the sheer joy of it. Having relinquished their former world, they have relinquished with it their identities. They share an anonymous solitude; where in 'Wants' Larkin sought an isolated oblivion, these horses have found a kind of oblivion in their anonymity and absence of memory. They now live in a continuous present, unplagued by the future (the prophecies of the stop-watch) or memories of the past. They live, too, in a close harmony with nature, merging with the shade, now knowing the 'unmolesting meadows', caught up in the slow, regular rhythm of the groom's arrival each evening, and so they live harmoniously by having relinquished identity, memory, anticipation. Unlike man they have no illusions, regrets, fears, doubts, even though the evening may be drawing to its ultimate close. The poem portrays a repose, a contentment, which brings *The Less Deceived* to a peaceful close tinged with melancholy, for these horses possess a tranquillity beyond humanity's grasp.

4.2 THE WHITSUN WEDDINGS

Here

The poem describes a journey to the north-east coast of England (near Hull, where Larkin lived latterly) and the different locales through which the poet passes, from 'rich industrial shadows', through the 'large town' (Hull itself) to a coastal 'beach/Of shapes and shingle'. It is a literal journey through a recognisably contemporary England; at the same time, the journey is also an imaginative flight away from modern urban materialism towards a vision of solitary freedom, 'unfenced existence', symbolised by the sea and sky stretching beyond the beach.

Having turned from 'traffic all night north', we leave behind an area of mass industrialisation (whose 'shadows' may sound sinister) and move into a partly rural landscape of 'skies and scarecrows, haystacks, hares and pheasants' before suddenly coming upon urban Hull with its 'domes and statues, spires and cranes'. Here is contemporary life at its most familiar, the 'cut-price crowd' gathering its household possessions with indiscriminating desire, for the seemingly random list which puts 'sharp shoes' next to 'iced lollies' suggests both how the eye is confused by the disorder and how this 'urban yet simple' crowd is devoted to objects (like the 'iced lollies') of only temporary gratification. The 'Pastoral' has given way to the crowded commercialism of 'ships up streets' and an always incomplete urban expansion with its 'mortgaged half-built edges'. But lying beyond the town are isolated villages and in contrast to the mechanised, impersonal town of 'flat-faced trolleys' the silent solitariness of the countryside 'clarifies' the sense of existence beyond the immediate: 'Here leaves unnoticed thicken,/Hidden weeds flower, neglected waters quicken'. Finally, beyond the cities, towns and villages, beyond all human habitation, the 'bluish neutral distance/Ends the land suddenly beyond a beach'. After its onward rush, the poem ends with a vision of finality, the ideal freedom of 'unfenced existence' symbolised by the unending sea invisible beyond the land. What lies physically beyond the shore also lies beyond our knowledge: it is 'untalkative, out of reach'. The poem progresses from the cramped and chaotic nature of modern life to a peaceful, almost inexpressible vision of expansiveness and release, a prospect of ultimate escape.

The poem's style is devoted to establishing a contrast between the restlessness of the first three stanzas and the tranquillity of the fourth. In a remarkable feat of syntactic control, Larkin makes the first sentence last twenty-four lines before suddenly pulling us up mid-way through the twenty-fifth. The contrasting brevity of 'Here silence stands/Like heat' mimes the sensation of a journey concluded, of arrival, silence, stillness (notice how the simile makes the silence itself tangible). That long opening sentence, uncoiling and itself 'swerving' throughout three stanzas, is a journey through a quick succession of realistic detail (as if glimpsed at speed) whilst the repeated conjunctions ('And traffic', 'And the widening river', 'And residents', 'And out beyond', 'And past') all of which come at the beginning of lines, create a surging, seemingly irresistible movement towards the sea at the poem's conclusion. The suspended present participle, 'Swerving', repeated throughout stanza one, is partly clinched by the verb 'Gathers' at the opening of stanza two, but the sentence is completely fulfilled only at the beginning of stanza three, so that the essential theme of the poem ('removed lives/Loneliness clarifies') is given weighty emphasis by the syntax, by the use of abstract words coming after all the concrete nouns of the first three stanzas and by the rhyming of 'lives' and 'clarifies'. The effect of all this is to create a mood of calm stillness in the final stanza following the hectic clutter of the first three.

The language brings together significant detail: for example, 'the slave museum' is both a historical monument and a quietly ironic reminder that in their own way 'grim head-scarfed wives' are themselves 'slaves' to a life-style they never chose. Within this realism, though, we find the language at crucial moments becoming more symbolically resonant. As the cities give way in the first stanza to 'solitude', the rhythm is quickened by the pleasantly alliterative 'skies and scarecrows, haystacks, hares and pheasants' before being retarded by the open vowels of 'widening river's slow pres-ence' (thus imitating the water's unhurried drift). As dawn breaks, the 'gold' clouds and 'shining' mud take on a luminous, almost other-worldly significance to be associated with the values of solitude. Similarly, when we reach the peace and isolation of the final stanza, we feel what it was never possible to feel in the town: the presence of a natural life which is almost hidden from us, 'unnoticed' and 'neglected'. This is emphasised by an image which is the opposite of absence, for '*Luminously-peopled* air ascends' (my italics): Larkin seems to suggest what is almost a paradox, that it is in states of solitariness that we become most vividly aware of other almost ghostly presences of non-human life and the lives lived by generations before us. The 'loneliness' of 'removed lives', the sense of solitary isolation, is celebrated by Larkin because only in this condition is one truly responsive to the pulse of life itself. The mass existence of the town is cramped and distracting. Here at the land's end, Larkin sees an alternative vision, one of 'unfenced existence'.

The poem expresses an abiding theme in Larkin's work. In 'Wants' (from his earlier collection, *The Less Deceived*) Larkin defines two funda-mental desires which lie beneath everything we do: 'the wish to be alone' and 'desire of oblivion'. In the same collection, 'Absences' portrays the surging movement of wind and sea and ends: 'Such attics cleared of me! Such absences!' Both poems show Larkin drawn towards conditions of emptiness, a vacancy in which no human figure, not even the poet's own presence, intrudes. The same attraction is evident in the conclusion of 'Here'. The final stanza celebrates stillness, silence and solitariness. Beyond the land we are confronted by the endless emptiness of sky and sea, the ideal vision of 'unfenced existence' which is 'untalkative' because of its own silence and because its significance is inexpressible. It is 'out of reach' of both the urban crowd caught up in its materialist desires and of the poet himself. 'Here' is finally beyond our gaze and our grasp, the infinity of space and time 'unfenced' by human knowledge and experience of it. And since this 'Here' is approached only at the end of a journey, its neutral vacancy and infinite nothingness seem to anticipate the state of death itself. The poet is irresistibly drawn to the ultimate silence and oblivion of mortality.

Mr Bleaney

Larkin has created in Mr Bleaney a character he disdains but fears he ma: too closely resemble. In five stanzas the outlines of Mr Bleaney's life a established, with its dull regularity and meagreness, before the two closing stanzas pass a general reflection both on the frightening emptiness of Mr Bleaney's life and on the speaker's implied similarity to him.

Mr Bleaney (the name itself suggests bleakness) was the previous tenant of the room which the poet is now to occupy, and the landlady's chatter, together with the details of the room which the poet quickly takes in, tell us a good deal about what sort of man he was. The room is cramped and bare (even the ashtray is makeshift) with nothing beyond its window but a patch of scrubland the landlady likes to call her garden (that Mr Bleaney took it 'properly in hand' is a lie calculated to pressurise the new tenant into doing so). There is no pretence at dignity: the curtains are tatty and shrunken, and their flowered pattern redolent of natural health and growth serves ironically to emphasise the bareness inside and outside the room. That same bareness was the essential quality of Mr Bleaney's life. The little incidentals of his existence as retailed by the landlady suggest a life of monotonous regularity, a habit of foolish expectancy (he played the football pools without ever winning) and, above all, loneliness (summer holidays spent at a quiet coastal resort and Christmas with his sister). For Mr Bleaney, life became a solitary emptiness occupied only by the meagre substance of habit.

But although the poet can infer a good deal about Mr Bleaney, the last two stanzas speculate on what the poet cannot know: how Mr Bleaney himself estimated his own life. If 'how we live measures our own nature', the conditions of dishevelled tedium in which Mr Bleaney lived should accurately reflect his true nature: he deserved no better than his down-at-heel solitariness. The drabness of his surroundings is an extension of the drabness of himself. His life seems to have been a failure that is reflected in the physical details of the room: it is dull (a 60-watt bulb), confined ('no room for books or bags') and stale (the bed is 'fusty'). The final stanza seems to assert that Mr Bleaney, being the sort of man he was, deserved no more than this 'hired box' of a room because he was incapable of achieving anything better.

It seems that the poet can feel nothing but contempt for his predecessor. The contemptuousness is felt in the disdainful listing of the meagre contents both of the room and of Mr Bleaney's routine and in the final claim that 'He warranted no better'. But if we attend to the tone of the final two stanzas more closely, what emerges is an attitude more complex than contempt. These concluding stanzas are marked off from the rest of the poem by their more complex syntax (they compose a lengthy sentence in contrast to the simpler phrases of the earlier stanzas) and by a shift in the diction towards a language more metaphorical ('frigid', 'Tousling') and abstract ('how we live measures our own nature'). These stanzas are more probing, more thoughtful than elsewhere in the poem because the poet is coming towards a recognition that the distinction he wants to make between himself and Mr Bleaney, the superiority of his contempt, is illusory. In occupying Mr Bleaney's room, he may be stepping into Mr

Bleaney's shoes. He may deserve no better than Mr Bleaney. His decision to take the room, in spite of its tawdriness, seems unpremeditated: ' "I'll take it" ' is blurted out impulsively. He now lies where Mr Bleaney lay, in the same 'cramped box', almost as if in a coffin. The merging of the poet with Mr Bleaney becomes closer when the poet attributes feelings to Mr Bleaney which are in fact his own. It is the poet who stands and watches 'the frigid wind/Tousling the clouds' (Mr Bleaney's imagination would not have been so vivid); it is the poet who lies on the bed trying to tell himself that 'this was home' but shivering at the rootless emptiness of his life; the poet who condemns himself by deciding that if 'how we live measures our own nature' then he does not add up to much. Beneath the offhand dismissal of Mr Bleaney, what the poet actually feels is a frightening similarity. By the end of the poem, the attitude that has emerged is not one of superiority, or even of pity. Almost unwillingly, the poet is drawn towards a recognition of himself in Mr Bleaney, a deeper self-knowledge which cuts through the illusion of superiority to the truth of his situation: in their drab isolation, he and Mr Bleaney are fellow-sufferers.

One of the most notable features of the poem is the way in which its meaning emerges by a slight change in tone. We begin with the landlady's compulsive chatter and move through the poet's weary familiarisation with the room and Mr Bleaney towards a conclusion which reveals more about the speaker than seems intended. Beneath the disdain for Mr Bleaney lies a hidden fear which, almost in spite of the speaker, surfaces at the poem's close to break the illusion of separateness between them. This irresistible pull towards a truth which the poem's speaker would rather avoid but cannot suppress is characteristic of Larkin.

Love Songs in Age

This poem takes up one of Larkin's abiding themes: the illusions with which we try to protect ourselves from a harsh reality. In this case, the illusion is that of love and the impossible demands we make of it. A trivial incident - a widow discovering old song-books - is examined to show how an insignificant experience can in fact reveal an inescapable truth.

The poem begins on a note of casual inconsequence. The song-books have been kept for no special reason, they have been carelessly treated (left in the sun, stained, scribbled on years ago by the widow's daughter) and they come to light now only by accident. There is a weightier significance, though, about the phrase 'So they had waited', as if there were something inevitable about their discovery. As the widow looks through them she is deeply moved by feelings of nostalgia as her past is vividly brought back to her. Now a widow, and her daughter grown up, she finds in the songs a freshly-created recollection of her youth. The musical chords are 'frank' and 'submissive' because they express simply an~ unquestioningly the clichés of sentimental love-songs. They bring wi~ them the energy and potential of youth, as when a tree begins to flou~

in spring, and its optimistic conviction that time is laid up in store and will never run out. But for the widow, time has run its course and that particular illusion has been shattered.

Rediscovering these songs is painful to her because an even greater illusion has been shattered since she first sang them. These love-songs remind her how love has failed to live up to its promise. The songs purvey a sentimental illusion: love is a 'glare', a 'much-mentioned brilliance' which sails above us out of reach: 'Still promising to solve, and satisfy,/ And set unchangeably in order'. The promises are not fulfilled: the songs, which present an image of love in which we like to believe, are lies. The widow closes the books recognising that the ideal of love portrayed by the songs and youthfully anticipated by her is an illusion. Love did not 'solve' all problems, 'satisfy' all her needs or give unfailing direction and purpose to her life. It is not that she has never felt love; rather, it is the sentimentally romantic image of it which invites disappointment by asking too much of love.

Clearly, this is a poem of disillusionment, and disillusion brings pain, as we see in the widow's tears. But the particular quality of 'Love Songs in Age' is its lack of bitterness when compared with other poems of disillusion such as 'Deceptions' or 'Dry-Point'. The woman recognises the disappointment inherent in confronting reality (love is not as we imagined it) but in being 'less deceived' she is not made cynical. The romanticised dreams of youthful courtship were put aside and neglected, as the books themselves were. Instead, the woman got on with the more modest achievements of domestic felicity: the books are marked by lying in the sun and by vases of flowers, both suggestive of warmth and fertility. Now the songbooks revive the old ideal of love in a surge of memories. But even as that ideal of love is described, Larkin's language indicates its dangerous illusoriness. A 'glare' which breaks out and sails above suggests an image of an uncomfortably strong sun which we cannot endure too long. In the same way, the romantic images of love in the songs make of love something too intense, too exhausting, too remote from us. This sort of love is 'incipient', always present but undeveloped, an ideal against which we measure our actual experience of love. That real experience may fall short of the ideal, but it may be the ideal we have of it which is the more damaging, not the more mundane experience of love we might have in the real world. The feeling expressed in the poem is thus not one of bitterness or cynicism that life fails our ideals of it, but of pathos, of a tender sympathy for the widow who recalls dreams knowing they are best forgotten.

Broadcast

arkin once described 'Broadcast' as the nearest he came to writing a love-
?m. At first sight it seems to affirm the tenderness of love but on closer
ing we should note how far it falls short of being an unqualified love-

The poet is listening to a broadcast on the radio of a concert his loved one is attending and as he listens to the music he tries to imagine her with an intensity that would bear witness to the depth of his feelings for her. As the broadcast begins, we hear the impersonal noises of a large audience preparing itself for the concert with its murmured chatter and nervous coughing, like a congregation at church ('Sunday-full') at its most respectful ('Organ-frowned-on'). A drum-roll introduces the national anthem, followed by the noise of a 'huge resettling' as the audience seats itself again. The music begins and the poet concentrates on summoning up the image of his loved one, 'Beautiful and devout', picked out from all the surrounding faces. At this stage, his impression of her seems sufficiently vivid for him to imagine even the glove she has accidentally dropped by her new but unfashionable shoes. In the gathering gloom of approaching winter ('it goes quickly dark') he continues to focus his attention on the radio whose light now glows in the darkness. But just as he loses sight of the 'Leaves on half-emptied trees', so he finds himself unwillingly distracted from concentrating on his beloved. The object of his devotion gradually recedes behind the music itself, obscured by 'rabid storms of chording'. Despite himself, the music overpowers his mind 'All the more shamelessly'. The music comes to him over a long distance and so he feels that he should be able to resist its intrusions easily. He is ashamed to find that it is the music in which he becomes engrossed, not his beloved who is attending the selfsame concert. When the music ends, he is left guiltily 'desperate to pick out' the woman's hands applauding, as if trying to compensate for his forgetfulness of her during the concert.

The poem develops complex feelings. The poet's tender regard for the woman is present in his solicitous concern for her dropped glove and the picking out of her face 'among all those faces'. But as the concert proceeds, so he is distracted from continuing his devotion to her. The music is increasingly overpowering even though the poet tries to resist its intrusiveness. It is described contemptuously as 'A snivel', then 'monumental slithering', 'rabid storms of chording' and finally a 'cut-off shout'. The degree of his contempt for the music intensifies but in doing so it only serves to show what a greater distraction the music becomes and how increasingly guilty he feels about losing his concentration on the woman.

During the concert, then, the woman fades from his mind until he guiltily recalls her at the end of the poem. Throughout the poem, though, his hold on her is precarious. The object of his love remains distant, removed, unspecified. The imagery of the gathering darkness itself suggests something fragile and vulnerable in their love. Just as he loses 'All but the outline of the still and withering/ Leaves on half-emptied trees', so the woman at the concert recedes from him. At the end of the poem, she remains only as 'hands, tiny in all that air'. She is surrounded by impersonal space, an impersonal audience (which the poet registers vaguely 'Giant whispering and coughing . . . and huge resettling') and is brought him through the electronic impersonality of the radio. The absorb tenderness of love which Larkin tries to capture in this poem is, we finally feel, only precariously achieved.

Faith Healing

We have seen how many of Larkin's poems explore the illusions by which we try to evade the uncomfortable truths of reality. One of those illusions is the illusion of love, which 'Love Songs in Age' portrayed as promising to end loneliness and confusion but inevitably failing in that promise. It is the eye of a satirist which exposes these illusions, for the satirist sets out to correct our failings by showing them to be absurd. But Larkin's poetry often stops short of satire and what prevents Larkin's satirical edge from biting too viciously is his compassion for the victims of illusion, a sympathy for those who undergo the pains of disillusionment, and a poignant yearning which wants our most precious illusions to be true. We can observe this balance between satire and sympathy in 'Faith Healing'.

The poem's scene is a faith-healing ceremony at which an evangelist promises to heal disabilities by the power of prayer and the blessing of divine love which is symbolised by the laying-on of his hands. The evangelist's outward appearance suggests reliability and wisdom: his spectacles, grey hair, dark suit and white collar give an air of 'Upright' trustworthiness. For the women who come to him he symbolises complete and overwhelming love. His 'deep American voice' is the comforting voice of a lover; his 'Now, dear child,/What's wrong', the words of a soothing mother, the clasping of their heads the firm protection of a father; above all, the evangelist's promise to perform miracles makes him a personal incarnation of God's divine and individual love. To what extent does Larkin ask us to believe in these various manifestations of love? Certainly, the women in the poem do, but Larkin's language suggests that we should not be so easily taken in. The evangelist's 'warm spring rain of loving care' (a suspiciously clichéd image) allows the women to 'dwell' with him only for some twenty seconds. He scarcely pauses between asking his solicitous question and launching into a prayer which, 'Directing God about this eye, that knee', seems oddly peremptory (who would 'direct' God?) and casually indiscriminate ('this eye, that knee'). Heads are clasped 'abruptly' before the women are 'exiled', some of them 'Sheepishly', as if almost ashamed of their credulity (the word also suggests how these women are led and manipulated like a flock of sheep).

Throughout this opening section, then, we can discern an ironic tone which tells us not to be taken in, as the women are, by the evangelist and is promise of transforming love. But the irony is stopped short of ckery. These women may be deluded into thinking that the evangelistic -healer can cure them of both their physical ailments and their al loneliness, but the deeply-felt intensity of their emotional out-hocks us into sympathy, not contempt. The irony which ridicules n in the first stanza suddenly evaporates when, in the second stanza, we are confronted by the anguish of the women's emotional release. Believing that they have now found a love which cares for them uniquely and individually, that their lives have acquired value and meaning, they are overcome by a joy so intense as to cause a physical reaction: 'some stay stiff, twitching and loud/With deep hoarse tears . . ./Their thick tongues blort, their eyes squeeze grief . . .'. The physical violence of these words shocks us out of our ironic aloofness. The faith-healer referred to each of them as 'dear child' and these women are indeed children, passive, obedient and in need of love. Encountering that love (however self-deceivingly), their response is that of a 'dumb/And idiot child', an inarticulate gush of gratitude and relief. What is wrong with them is not their physical ailments: 'By now, all's wrong'. They are life's casualties. 'Moustached in flowered frocks', they are lonely, unloved and unlovely. Now, the child in them which wants to believe that the world is good surfaces 'To re-awake at kindness'. Larkin makes it clear that this is a momentary illusion by portraying them as children. Their eyes 'squeeze grief' because fundamentally they know that they are indulging an illusion, an illusion which is nonetheless irresistible and universal: 'In everyone there sleeps/A sense of life lived according to love'. Some of their own lives might have been different had they loved others, 'but across most it sweeps/As all they might have done had they been loved'. As in 'Love Songs in Age', love is imagined as a transforming power which might give life meaning and purpose. These women represent all of us, trapped by a sense of fulfilment and perfection which we cannot ignore ('the voice above/Saying *Dear child*,') but cannot make real, for 'time has disproved' our ideals. We know they are illusions, but we are powerless either to resist them or to translate them into reality.

What, finally, is our reaction to these women? The poem begins by making them look foolish, willing participants in a calculated illusion, as 'Stewards tirelessly/Persuade them onwards'. We take the side of the poet, feeling superior to the women in our scepticism. But then we are shocked into sympathy. Their unrestrained, unembarrassed outpouring of joy and grief moves us towards a recognition of a shared condition. We share with these women an inherent longing for ideals which always escape us but which we cannot stop ourselves pursuing even though we are doomed to disappointment and disillusionment. Indeed, without a momentary faith in these illusions we would be unremittingly confronted by the essential emptiness and futility of our condition. The poem charts, convincingly and movingly, a shift of attitude from ironic detachment to compassion.

Toads Revisited

As the title suggests, this poem is a companion-piece to 'Toads' (in *The Less Deceived*). In that earlier poem, we saw how Larkin uses a speaking voice to betray itself into revealing more than it intended. The speaker began by expressing envy for a free-wheeling life-style shorn of all responsibility. But that envy is revealed as a pretence trying to obscure more deep-seated sense of moral superiority. The speaker actually prefers his own humdrum way of life. It leaves him free to enjoy the possibility that he might throw it all off whilst knowing that because he despises those who live irresponsibly he himself never will give up work. The process of rationalisation leads to a conclusion which does not reflect much credit on the speaker, for there is a self-regarding complacency about his feelings of superiority. In 'Toads Revisited', the speaker again defends his routine way of life. But this time the self-justification occurs not by the sifting and probing of attitudes, but by the speaker recognising (as in 'Faith Healing') a common predicament shared with those he despises.

The opening tone of voice is typically conversational, off-the-cuff, the half-rhymes and relaxed three-stress lines helping to create a casual ease. The tone shifts at the first full rhyme ('be/me') as the speaker expresses his discomfort at taking time off work to stroll around the park. He does not like 'Being one of the men/You meet of an afternoon', and this vague unease is sharpened by the list which follows, for the sort of men who can waste their afternoons are all blighted in some way. They are not carefree (as in 'Toads') or heroic adventurers (as in 'Poetry of Departures'). They have not chosen a way of life; life has had its own way with them. Where 'Poetry of Departures' had its hero 'swagger the nut-strewn roads', we now find 'Palsied old step-takers'; the virile hero 'Stubbly with goodness' is now 'Waxed-fleshed'. All these characters in 'Toads Revisited' are victims, not protagonists; victims of age, or neurosis, or accident, or impoverishment. They have no personality and only a minimal hold on life: they are 'vague' and 'in long coats' as if shrouded. The speaker's attitude hardens into bigoted disdain: these men dodge work and responsibilities by being 'stupid or weak'. But as he imagines the drifting emptiness of their lives he finds himself drawn towards sympathy: 'Turning over their failures . . . No friends but empty chairs'.

Now he can emphatically endorse his own choice of a busy, ordered, respectable life of duty and work and the rhythmical pace quickens energetically:

> No, give me my in-tray,
> My loaf-haired secretary,
> My shall-I-keep-the-call-in-Sir . . .

But there is a lack of conviction in this surge of enthusiasm. In order to defend his own way of life, the speaker has chosen to compare himself with life's most unfortunate victims, suggesting there is not much he dare praise in his own life. When it comes to asserting the value of his own existence, three brisk lines containing images of bare routine succeed only in exposing its underlying emptiness. Given the choice between his own way of life and that of 'the men/You meet of an afternoon', he will of course choose his own: 'What else can I answer,/When the lights come on four/At the end of another year?' Just as the men in the park seemed to victims, enduring a life they had not chosen, so the poet himself finds his own existence drifting out of his control, years slipping away as swiftly as the hours in a day. Ultimately, he and the casualties in the park are the same, surviving a bleak existence whose end is the same for all of them: 'Give me your arm, old toad;/Help me down Cemetery Road'. If the speaker finally opts for a life of conventional respectability, he does so knowing that his choice is ineffectual, for he is as much a victim of chance and circumstance as the men in the park, his destiny in the cemetery as inescapable for him as it is for them. In the end, he must accept the 'toad' of work and responsibility simply as a means of helping him endure life. It is not something which confers superiority or makes him essentially different from those he would like to despise in order to justify himself.

Water

'Water' reveals an aspect of Larkin's poetry which is frequently overlooked. The poems for which he is best known refer to a recognisably 'real' world of towns and trains, advertising hoardings and municipal parks. Other poems chart the progress of a mind in debate with itself, arguing, rationalising, concluding. Their language refers us to everyday experiences and situations, to a familiar reality. But there are a few poems where Larkin uses language rather differently, to create metaphors and images and extend them or juxtapose them surprisingly. This technique owes something to the symbolist procedures of some late nineteenth-century French poets and their twentieth-century successors such as T. S. Eliot and W. B. Yeats in England and Ireland. In these poems our attention is directed not so much to the things named by words as to the words themselves, their sounds and connotations, the metaphors and images which words can create however remote such images are from actual 'real' existence. There are many things about this way of writing of which Larkin disapproves – symbolist poems can be difficult and ultimately incomprehensible – but there have been occasions when Larkin has written in a symbolist manner. 'Water' is one of them. Water is associated in all religions and rituals with cleansing, purification and rebirth and it is these associations gathering around the word which Larkin invokes in his poem

The opening makes clear that he is not a 'believer' in any one religion; he would have to 'construct' one himself 'if' he were 'called in' – a remote possibility. We are presented, then, with a temperament sceptical about established religions but responsive to a central image of religion. But his religion would 'make use' of water not just as an image, but as a tangible reality (which many religions do, for example, in baptism). Going to church would be a 'fording', a literal wading through water entailing a change of clothes. Larkin means this both literally and metaphorically; metaphorically, it reminds us of baptism as a symbol of cleansing and a rite of passage into a new spiritual state which might actually change one existence (as Larkin's congregation would have to put on 'dry, differe clothes'). Water would be central to the poet's religious language practices, involving an enthusiastic 'sousing' and 'furious devout drench'. The final stanza explains the imaginative importance of water to the poet. Raising a glass of water is a simple act of homage, as when the priest raises the consecrated host. The east is where the sun rises, suggestive of warmth and life's reawakening. The sun's rays would be caught and intensified by the water, 'Where any-angled light/Would congregate endlessly'. 'Congregate' has an obvious religious association, but this final, cumulative image transfigures the ordinariness of water into magnificence. The water gathers and contains 'any-angled' light in an all-inclusive embrace, 'endlessly'. The poem ends with an imaginative apprehension of infinity, timelessness and completeness. It does so with an image of radiance, with sun and water celebrated as elemental presences which in Larkin's imagination suggest a spiritual existence outside the constraints of destructive time and material reality. This poem, like 'Here', apprehends 'unfenced existence . . . out of reach'. It does so by taking the mundane image of water and using its traditional religious associations to converge upon a final image of startling simplicity and resonance.

The Whitsun Weddings

This is one of the most widely anthologised and best-known poems written in England since 1945. Its appeal derives from its faithful representation of familiar experiences: a hot day's train journey, the landscapes of post-industrial England, the noise and bustle of wedding-parties at railway stations, the gradual shift from specific observation to general reflection. There is too a remarkable technical control of language in which we find a careful development of feeling and attitude. The poem has secured for itself a significant place in the tradition of English poetry.

The subject of the poem is a train journey from the North of England to London and the poet's observation of the various wedding-parties he sees boarding the train at different stations on the way. We begin with the remarkable recreation of the sensations of travelling by train on a summer's day: the heat, the relief after the rush to catch the train ('all sense/Of being in a hurry gone'), the snapshot details viewed through the carriage window as the town gives way to countryside. Larkin's description accurately captures the speaker's mechanical registration of fleeting detail: the backs of houses, the street of 'blinding windscreens', the smell of the fish-dock all flash by too quickly to engage anything more than a vague interest, until we see the river's estuary when the poem's rhythm slows to catch the sensation of amplitude and tranquillity, 'Where sky and Lincolnshire and water meet'. The second stanza continues the journey inland 'through the tall eat that slept/For miles. . .'. The poet's senses are engaged but not wholly sorbed in his observations, for he is of course isolated in the train from world outside it, and that world is presented to him in a fleeting sequence ıages framed by a window. He watches, but is uninvolved, and we in the succession of details in this stanza a hint of boredom in the speaker. Nevertheless, Larkin presents to us a familiar and recognisable English landscape that varies from 'Wide farms' to 'Canals with floatings of industrial froth' and the featureless appearance of new towns 'Approached with acres of dismantled cars'.

The third stanza introduces a growing alertness and responsiveness to the scene around the speaker. He is roused from his reading and the drowsiness of heat and sunshine by the noise and colour of a wedding-party on the shaded platform, struck for the first time on this journey by something that seems to have significance. The girls 'posed irresolutely', waving their farewells to the married couple on the train, are signalling both a conclusion and a beginning, 'As if out on the end of an event/Waving goodbye/ To something that survived it'. Now the poet's interest is caught he is more curious and sees the next wedding-party 'in different terms', not quite so vaguely and with a growing scepticism. His description of perspiring fathers with 'seamy foreheads; mothers loud and fat;/An uncle shouting smut' indicates his distaste for the jaunty vulgarity of the occasion. The women are gaudy in their cheap finery which marks them off 'unreally from the rest' and the occasion itself is tawdry ('banquet-halls up yards, and bunting-dressed/Coach-party annexes'); advice is thrown as inconsequentially as confetti. Now observing the scene more closely but still with a detached aloofness, the poet sees what the event has signified to the participants: the children's boredom; the fathers' swaggering self-importance; the women's knowingness, sharing 'The secret like a happy funeral' and the younger girls' uneasy sombreness.

Returning his attention to the new occupants of the train, the poet's tone shifts again. He is now aware of how all these newly-wed couples are sharing this journey and is struck by the thought that for a brief moment each of these couples is united in a common experience. It is an experience which now partly includes the speaker; no longer a spectator, he has become closer to a participant, and this is shown in his use of the first person plural, 'We hurried towards London', and in his anticipating what the dozen couples will say of this journey in the future. The landscape they watch is one he watches too, and although 'none/Thought of the others they would never meet/Or how their lives would all contain this hour', the poet himself escapes this self-absorption and becomes their representative in recognising and memorialising this moment for them.

Having recognised how the dozen couples are now assimilated with him in this journey, the speaker's attitude is developed. A poem that began with his sense of isolation, then amused detachment shifting to distaste and now a closer involvement, ends with moving compassion. As the train rushes into London past 'walls of blackened moss' which seem to draw perilously close, the speaker is suddenly aware of the future's potential contained in this moment on this train 'ready to be loosed with all the power/That being changed can give'. These dozen couples have undergone a ritual which marks a change in their lives, a new beginning. As the train slows, the sensation of falling suggests to Larkin an image of launching, as if this shared journey is the impetus which will project these new lives into their separate futures:

> We slowed again,
> And as the tightened brakes took hold, there swelled
> A sense of falling, like an arrow-shower
> Sent out of sight, somewhere becoming rain.

The image of the 'arrow-shower' is complex. Rain does not fall in a parabolic curve and what Larkin is asking us to imagine is a flight of arrows (a 'shower') which falls out of sight, somewhere in the future, as rain. 'Arrows' might suggest Cupid's darts; less fancifully, Larkin uses the metaphor of arrows to extend the image of lives being projected from the present into the future. That it is an image of procreation and growth is made clear by the 'shower . . . rain' metaphor of fertility. This is the power 'That being changed can give': the progress towards happiness and fulfilment is undertaken even if its achievement is 'out of sight', unforeseeable and uncertain.

This is one of Larkin's most celebratory poems, although some critics have argued that the final image is one of foreboding. It is true that the speaker at first regards the weddings with suspicion and even patronising haughtiness. But Larkin's language makes clear that this is not his final view of the marriages. The couples are 'Free at last' and there is a sense of abundance in their being 'loaded with the sum of all they saw'. This journey is for them a moment of transition between past and future; the 'end of an event' has given way to the 'something that survived it'. Their journey is incomplete, for although the train may stop in London their lives, all containing this hour, take off from there. This sense of incompleteness is caught even in the description of what they see: the cricketer 'running up to bowl', an incomplete action, foreshadows the image of the arrow-shower. Moreover, when the poet thinks of London lying ahead of them 'spread out in the sun,/Its postal districts packed like squares of wheat', the image again suggests fertility, abundance, sustenance (the borough boundaries on a map look like densely-packed cornfields seen from above) and the use of 'swelled' in the final sentence similarly suggests plenitude. The poem is not so sentimental as to suggest that these couples will find contentment. Rather, the journey itself is used as a metaphor for time and change. The marriage ceremonies are a symbolic expression of change, a change which has the 'power' to create a future for itself, just as the train's journey is a succession of different images from one moment to the next. Of course, the speaker is not a full participant in this change that has been chosen by the married couples around him. But a journey that began with the poet's purely mechanical interest in what lay outside him ends with a positive affirmation of the human capacity to change the direction of life, even if that direction cannot itself be determined.

The poem's real triumph, though, is in the mastery of language by which the shape and feel of experience are precisely rendered. The regularity of rhyme and rhythm helps to create a sense of inevitability, a pattern of movement. The landscapes of contemporary England are observed with delicate precision. Notice the vivid compactness which makes a hot-house flash 'uniquely', where that surprisingly abstract word seems inevitable and just in suggesting the momentary alignment of sun, glass and observer. Similarly, in the final stanza the train is described as a 'frail/Travelling coincidence', reminding us not only how closely it approaches the encroaching walls, but also how accidentally and arbitrarily these couples happen to be gathered together on this train, how each moment in our lives is 'a frail/Travelling coincidence' brought about by chance. At the end of the poem, our literal falling-forward as a train slows towards a stop is converted into a metaphor expressing how the future is unpredictably launched from the present. The pause in the run-on line between 'swelled' and 'A sense of falling' itself imitates that sense of falling. This ability to capture physical sensation can also be seen in 'the tall heat that slept/For miles inland', conveying the claustrophobic stillness and numbing drowsiness of a hot summer's day. We will see that there are more sombre, bleaker poems in *The Whitsun Weddings* when Larkin seems overwhelmed by futility and inertia, by a sense of defeat. But the poems themselves, as with this title poem, represent a triumph of artistry over life. If the poet commands little else in life, he can command language.

MCMXIV

In this poem, Larkin looks back to a distant and simpler age, a time of 'innocence' before the modern nightmare began. He pictures England as it was in 1914 at the outbreak of the First World War at the moment when, according to the orthodoxies of modern history, everything was to change utterly. The carnage of that war was yet to be unleashed; after it came the political, social and intellectual upheavals which characterise our own age. The Roman numerals of the title immediately suggest how remote that pre-1914 era now seems, as remote and irrecoverable as the ancient civilisations of Greece and Rome.

In the opening stanza the men who wait cheerfully to volunteer do not know yet of the horror awaiting them in the trenches. For them, the war is an adventure, a sport not very different from a football or cricket match (hence the references to the Oval and Villa Park – a London cricket ground and a Birmingham football stadium). It is the coming experience of that war which separates us from them and which determined that nothing could be the same again. Even the men's faces now look different, 'moustached' and 'archaic'. The physical details of a street-scene summon up a bygone era: sunblinds are 'bleached', as if durably well-worn through long, hot summers; the 'Established names' refers to the once common practice of dating a shop's origin along with its title; 'farthings and sovereigns' name a currency now outdated. This second stanza creates a picture of 1914 and notes everything that makes it different from today: children in modest, soberly dark clothes, named respectfully after the era's heroes (its imperial royalty, not the fleeting 'stars' of fashion) and adverts made out of tin for such homely and everyday products as cocoa and tobacco (compare this with the garish contemporary advertising in 'Sunny Prestatyn').

In the countryside, the threat of war and change is even more distant. Larkin describes it as 'not caring', conveying with brilliant economy his sense of that era's carefree security. Place-names are left to become obscured by wild flowers because for a settled population there was no need for them; landholdings remain intact from William the Conqueror's Domesday Book, and the 'wheat's restless silence' beautifully captures the feeling of peaceful bounty. Class distinctions were durable and accepted, and the dust thrown up from untreated roads behind 'limousines' (the word is deliberately old-fashioned) is the dust of a past that still clung to the way of life that was led in 1914. Here is an existence of undisturbed calm, rooted in custom and tradition.

But the final stanza expresses a wistful nostalgia for a past which seems no longer to belong to us. The repetition of 'Never' at the beginning of three lines is like a funeral bell tolling for a vanished age. The quality of that age which has disappeared and for which Larkin yearns is 'innocence': not only the unwitting innocence with which men left homes and wives to which they were never to return, but the 'innocence' of a way of life free from the commercialism, instability and restlessness of contemporary life which lacks the assurance of settled values. Suddenly, 'Without a word', that era vanished from us, 'changed itself to past' and was never to be resumed. Silently, without our knowing it, history propelled us into our modern world of confusion, doubt and anxiety.

The poem is remarkable for its creation of a mood of poignant mourning and regret. This is achieved by its loving enumeration of detail: the poem is a single sentence which lingers over the features of a photograph (real or imagined), moving slowly and with quiet ease from men to shops to children, to advertisements, to the countryside, to servants and to cars. The effect of this slowly uncoiling sentence is one of stillness, as if Larkin tries to freeze-frame the onward progression of history. His poem is an attempt to preserve a particular moment before it suddenly changes, and that moment is itself celebrated because it belongs to an age of preservation when change was itself a slow process. Each stanza contains only one full rhyme and this helps to create the feeling of unhurried flow, of relaxed tranquillity. The final stanza returns us to the present and the abrupt last line has a piercing pathos:

> Never such innocence again.

Talking in Bed

This is another poem in which Larkin explores the difficulty and the ultimate futility inherent in human relations. A couple lying together in bed, as they have done for years, seems to represent an intimacy and honesty that is complete. Yet the poem goes on to suggest that even in the physical closeness of lovers, true unity and understanding remain beyond us.

The first stanza begins with a simple declaration: 'Talking in bed ought to be easiest'; if ever human beings are to be genuinely close and self-revelatory then it should be in this situation – 'An emblem of two people being honest'. But through a sequence of images, Larkin suggests why it is that 'more and more time passes silently'. It is as if the lovers' ears are attuned to 'Outside', not to each other, listening only to the wind whose 'incomplete unrest' mirrors their own condition of unsettled incompleteness. The wind 'Builds and disperses clouds about the sky', ceaselessly roaming, changing, shifting, reflecting the unfinished ebb and flow of the lovers' feelings for one another. The 'dark towns' of which the lovers are distractingly aware 'heap up on the horizon' in a way suggesting random purposelessness, as if the world is governed by accidental and capricious forces – forces which have brought these lovers together arbitrarily. And this world outside is indifferent, hostile and impersonal: 'None of this cares for us'. The motion of the wind and the clouds, the sprawling mass of the towns, all seem incalculable, inexplicable. In a universe without reason 'Nothing shows why' things are as they are, or why the lovers should be unable to achieve complete harmony and unity. In bed together, they should be at the furthest point from loneliness, 'this unique distance from isolation', and yet 'It becomes still more difficult to find/Words at once true and kind'. This rhyming couplet disconcertingly asserts that what might be 'true' is very different from what would be 'kind', that 'truth' and 'kindness' are mutually exclusive. The final line is even bleaker: 'Or not untrue and not unkind.' The problem has suddenly become not one of expressing both truth and kindness, but of positively avoiding deception and cruelty. The lovers in their bed not only fail to be honest and gentle with each other; they fail to avoid the opposite, mutual deception and bitterness. And with this final line we become aware of a grim pun at the poem's opening, for 'Lying together' is what these lovers have inevitably done.

The repeated double negative of the final line is bleakly pessimistic; in a poem expressing the absence of our capacity for mutual involvement, those double negatives are cruelly appropriate (in a way which recalls the repeated negatives and 'unspent' childhood of 'I Remember, I Remember'). The lovers of this poem are unspecified and unlocalised; lying in bed, their imaginations are occupied only by the awareness of 'Outside', not each other. They remain apart, individual, solitary, sharing only their essential human condition of lonely isolation.

The Large Cool Store

As elsewhere in Larkin's poems, we enter the world of commercialised dreams in 'The Large Cool Store'. One section of the supermarket caters for the humdrum, workaday world of shift-work in factories and the daily grind of labour. But another section of the store entertains our dreams of feminine beauty and eroticism, dreams which Larkin once again reveals as illusions, an ideal beyond our attainment.

The 'cheap clothes/Set out in simple sizes plainly' with their dull colours summon up the routine, practical necessity of work. Beyond this reminder of ordinariness, though, we find a display of women's nightwear which Larkin's language elevates to an almost ethereal status. Shirts and trousers are in 'heaps', but 'Modes For Night' (an advertiser's euphemism) 'Spread' like flowers in bloom. Their colours, 'Lemon, sapphire, moss-green, rose' are suggestive of natural growth and precious jewellery; they 'Flounce in clusters' in a sexually playful manner ('clusters' also sustains the image of diamonds).

These thin, light, diaphanous nightdresses seem to have no connection with the functional clothes of 'the weekday world'. They seem to have been designed for an image which does not exist in reality but only in our imagination. The image of women they represent is unearthly: 'Baby-Dolls', wispy almost fairy-like creatures, are simply not to be found in workaday reality. For Larkin, these 'Modes For Night' are a symptom of a masculine dream, the dream of perfect angelic beauty. They are a testament to 'How separate and unearthly love is,/Or women are, or what they do' because they purvey an ideal and hence false version of femininity which belongs to 'our young unreal wishes'. These clothes perpetuate an adolescent, immature vision of womanhood as 'synthetic, new,/And natureless in ecstasies'. 'Synthetic' implies the falsehood of that vision; 'natureless' suggests how that view of women is utterly divorced from reality and truth. The ideal remains in our imagination, bolstered by the manipulative images created by advertisers. As in 'Love Songs in Age', love is shown as a misguided attempt to incarnate a dream, an ideal. 'Natureless', that sort of love is doomed to disappointment and disillusionment.

Larkin is not necessarily asking us to disapprove of the commercial exploitation of our fantasies. Rather, he accepts that these cheap nightgowns express a natural desire to escape from the reality we know, the reality of 'low terraced houses . . . factory, yard and site'. But in attempting to rise above that reality, we can experience only the pain of disappointment for experience teaches that our dreams are by definition 'natureless'. The naivety of supposing that women resemble our fantasy-versions of them is caught in the nursery-rhyme-like simplicity of the poem's rhyme-scheme (a/b/a/b/a) and jogging tetrameters (four stresses to the line). The bathetic rhyme between 'Shorties' and 'sort is' (almost as absurd as that between 'poster...coast, a' in 'Sunny Prestatyn') points up how ridiculous are 'our young unreal wishes'.

Ambulances

One of Larkin's most assured poems, 'Ambulances' moves from the specific experience of seeing an ambulance to a general reflection probing the significance of our response.

Larkin's ambulances, suggestive of disaster and emergency, are secretive and mysterious, closed off from the outside world 'like confessionals', a place where one confronts one's deepest nature. They are private, self-absorbed, their darkened windows returning no reflections. Their calls are random and ubiquitous; visiting 'any kerb' and 'all streets' they are reminders of our own mortality. The first stanza presents ambulances as impersonal, frightening messengers of unpredictable fate. Onlookers find themselves randomly caught up in somebody else's loss and tragedy, accidental spectators of 'A wild white face' which interrupts their mundane routine. For a moment, normal life stands still with children caught 'strewn' across the road and women leaving their shopping and cooking. As they watch the stretcher 'stowed' in the ambulance, they momentarily sense the tenuousness of their own lives. The immediate presence of death brings to the surface of their awareness 'the solving emptiness/That lies just under all we do'. For a second, they are vividly conscious of their own mortality, the blank, infinite emptiness of death which could at any moment dissolve their own lives and which one day will strike them. So when they whisper *'Poor soul'* they are in fact pitying themselves, suddenly made aware of the unpredictable inevitability of their own deaths.

The fourth stanza develops their sense of inherent extinction. The ambulance drives off in 'deadened air' and its shut doors bring almost to a close a unique, individual life. The constituent elements of that life, all its accidental, unforeseen and haphazard events, its self-made continuity, 'the unique random blend/Of families and fashions' finally begin to come apart. The interwoven strands which composed that particular life now unravel as death begins to nullify the individual life carried away in the ambulance. The 'white face' is now 'Far/From the exchange of love', its existence no longer corroborated by a partner as it now lies 'Unreachable', remote and separate. Watching the ambulance, we are brought closer to the nothingness of our own death. It 'dulls to distance all we are' in confronting us with the essential, inescapable reality of death. The living identity we feel ourselves to have and which is given substance by our daily habits and behaviour suddenly perishes in the face of death's continuous presence. Ambulances confront us with 'what is left to come': our own death.

The meaning of the poem may be disconcerting but hardly original. That is not Larkin's intention: he uses a familiar incident – an ambulance in an emergency dash through the traffic – to articulate and clarify our common response. But if the poem is not original in proffering the thought that ambulances frighten us, we can nevertheless admire Larkin's skilful and economical use of language.

We begin with a surprising simile, 'Closed like confessionals', which brings to mind the solemn, unearthly silence within the ambulance contrasting with the 'Loud noons of cities' outside. The ambulances 'thread'

in an intricate, mechanically impersonal way across the city, disconnected
from the bustling life around them. But they are also a chilling part of our
civic order, uniformly painted with 'arms on a plaque'. The line about
women hurrying 'Past smells of different dinners' vividly roots us in an
everyday normality which seems to bear no relation to the frightening
'wild white face that overtops/Red stretcher-blankets'. The stretcher is
'stowed' in the ambulance, and the word forcibly emphasises the dehu-
manised nature of this moment. As the ambulance disappears, Larkin
explores our reaction to such an incident. We are distressed not by some-
one else's accident, but because we have been sharply reminded that our
own lives might at any moment be so finally unravelled. Suddenly, every-
thing we are, everything we have done, is threatened by the final nullity
of death. The pattern of our lives, what made it 'cohere', is so easily frac-
tured and the consciousness of this makes our own lives vulnerable and
fragile. This ambulance simply attends the final accident in the series of
accidents which make up the 'unique random blend' we call life. Larkin's
merging in these final two stanzas of abstract and concrete language (so
that the abstraction of 'unique random blend' is given a tangible concrete-
ness by the metaphor of 'cohered. . .loosen') is moving and masterly. The
poem is structurally regular and closely-knit. The five stanzas follow a
simple a/b/c/b/c/a rhyme-scheme, so that the central four lines have the
interlinked firmness of the traditional alternately-rhymed quatrain. This,
together with the regular iambic tetrameter, gives the poem a solidity
which challenges the dissolution of death. The poem's generalisations thus
possess a tone of stately gravity and urgent seriousness:

> And sense the solving emptiness
> That lies just under all we do,
> And for a second get it whole,
> So permanent and blank and true.

Sunny Prestatyn

Like 'The Large Cool Store', this poem deals with the way in which we
torment ourselves with images that we cannot translate into reality. As
in other poems, Larkin employs the unreal images created by advertisers to
measure the distance between their idealised vision of perfection and the
bleaker, dishevelled world we actually inhabit. 'Sunny Prestatyn' is another
poem of disillusionment.

The first stanza presents us with the picture of an advertisement extol-
ling the attractions of Prestatyn, a Welsh coastal resort. The image is cal-
culated to suggest blissful and carefree excitement and at its centre is the
tantalising promise of sex. The girl on the poster revealingly clad in 'tautened
white satin' (suggestive of virginal purity) so dominates the image that the
coastline and hotel behind her 'Seemed to expand from her thighs', and
everything in the poster is arranged to emphasise the eroticism of her

'breast-lifting arms'. The 'hunk of coast' suggests a masculine strength; the 'Hotel with palms' an erotic Eden where every wish might be fulfilled. Notice how the stanza gradually builds up to the awed delight of 'breast-lifting arms'. The first thing we take in is the girl's expression of laughter; then our eye travels from her kneeling position to the thighs which seem to overwhelm the background detail and is finally arrested by the lifted breasts. The rhyme and rhythm help to convey an increasing excitement. The second sentence of this first stanza mimics with comic exaggeration the enraptured tones of a speaking voice. That audacious rhyme between 'poster' and 'coast, a' suggests a momentarily-held breath before the voice plunges on in exhilaration until the slow, open vowels of the last line with its lyrical promise of plenitude.

The second stanza suddenly punctures this larger-than-life image with the casual brusqueness of 'She was slapped up one day in March' before detailing the deformities and obscenities which within a fortnight now bedeck the poster. The language becomes deliberately blunt and crude: breasts now become 'tits', her 'crotch' is 'fissured' and the girl is set astride 'cock and balls' made even uglier by the adjective 'tuberous'. Larkin's language is here calculated to shock us out of the illusion represented by the poster, an illusion 'too good for this life'. Its exaggerated promise is false and our sympathies are directed to the graffitist whose obscenities register the frustrated disillusionment of the real world. 'Titch Thomas' refused to be taken in by the poster, and his defacement of it is more than gratuitous vandalism. The knife that has cruelly stabbed 'right through/ The moustached lips of her smile' punctures an inflated dream-world by which the advertiser's image would attempt to deceive us. Both Larkin and 'Titch Thomas' respond to the romantic appeal of the poster before recognising it as a dangerous, unattainable illusion which only creates unfulfillable expectations of life. 'Titch Thomas' and the poet are the less deceived and the less deceiving; the real obscenity lies with the creators of such images who knowingly exploit our fantasies in a callous pretence that they can be turned into reality. The new poster ('*Fight Cancer*') returns us more honestly to our bleaker, grimmer reality.

The force of the poem lies in the contrast between the dream-world of the poster and the earthy violence of its defacement leading to the quiet resignation of the poem's last sentence. The language used by Larkin to describe the poster is tinged with irony and a comic playfulness which makes fun of the advertiser's clichés: the girl's 'white satin', her expansive thighs and breasts. This mockery, though, is intensified by the crude slang of the second stanza which robs the advertiser's image of its beguiling, deceptive appeal, and bludgeons it into conforming with reality.

First Sight

This poem is a fine example of Larkin's linguistic artistry. Its design is symmetrical: two stanzas of exactly similar sentence length, each stanza alternately rhymed before concluding with a couplet. This architectural balance helps to give the poem its air of careful gravity which is reinforced by the steady tetrameter (four strong beats) of the rhythm.

The first stanza describes lambs newly-born in winter. Larkin's language brilliantly conveys the hostile world into which they are born, its 'vast unwelcome', the 'sunless glare' and the 'wretched width of cold'. We again see here that combination of abstract and concrete language which conveys experience with exactness and precision. 'Vast' suggests the endlessly inhospitable infinity of a landscape covered in snow, a world which nowhere affords shelter or comfort. 'Sunless glare' again emphasises the hostility of the landscape, the painful dazzle of the snow combined with the bleak coldness of 'sunless'. The 'wretched width of cold' captures the sense of almost agoraphobic exposure to the inescapable cold. These images are brilliantly compact, conveying their impressions with crystal vividness.

The second stanza shifts us away from the lambs and the snow to what lies invisible from sight: 'Earth's immeasurable surprise'. Hidden not only from sight, but also from understanding ('They could not grasp it if they knew') lurks the future: spring and the infinite cycle of time. What awaits is 'Utterly unlike the snow', utterly unlike the present, unforeseeable and beyond control. That future is perpetually beyond us, both in terms of our ability to fashion it ('grasp it') and beyond us in time, 'so soon' but never 'now'. The image of 'wake and grow' suggests spring, but also the 'immeasurable surprise' of future experience.

We might clarify our understanding of this poem by comparing it with an earlier one (in *The Less Deceived*) which takes up a similar theme. 'Wires' describes how 'Young steers', 'scenting purer water' beyond the electric fences blunder up against them and suffer their 'muscle-shredding violence'. Suddenly pained, 'Young steers become old cattle from that day', having learned to keep within 'Electric limits'. The poem suggests that experience constrains us within habitual routine: if we dare to 'stray' beyond familiar boundaries we risk pain. Will the same happen to Larkin's lambs (themselves suggestive of innocence) in 'First Sight'? The poem seems more optimistic in associating their future, their 'immeasurable surprise', with spring. What awaits them is beneficent, benign. But as these lambs mature, what they will experience will be the recurring cycle of the seasons, a pattern of repetition. 'First Sight' will not last long: soon it will be the hindsight of familiarity and experience. Spring 'lies/Hidden round them, waiting too' and there is a suggestion here of something lurking, threatening and menacing. The threat is in the inevitable fact that spring will be a 'surprise' only once; after that, experience will make it stale and familiar and any attempt to escape familiarity will result in the painful shock that befalls the young steers in 'Wires'. The innocence of the lambs is temporary; soon, life will inevitably take on the colourless, bleak uniformity of the winter landscape into which they were born. Only on 'first sight' does the future seen an 'immeasurable surprise'; after that, it shrinks to the repetition of disappointment and constriction. Herein lies the pathos of the poem: there can only ever be one 'first sight' before the future stales into familiarity. But the poem keeps a poised balance between hope and the unspoken logic of disillusionment, between concrete impressions ('Her fleeces wetly caked') and vivid abstraction ('Earth's immeasurable surprise').

Dockery and Son

One of Larkin's most important poems, 'Dockery and Son' (the very title suggests the established continuity of a family firm) meditates on the futility of the choices we make in life and asserts that life composes a pattern beyond our control or will.

The occasion for these reflections is the speaker's return to his old college. What should be an opportunity for self-indulgent nostalgia turns out to be a disappointment and a threat. The first stanza develops the speaker's sense of isolation. He is an outsider even in his former college; an outsider, in fact, from his own past. He is uncomfortably 'Death-suited, visitant', and when he tries the door of where he used to live it is significantly locked. Once familiar lawns are now 'dazzlingly wide'. He catches his train 'ignored' and watches his past disappear: 'Canal and clouds and colleges subside', wherein the alliteration emphasises a slightly bitter mood of pretended indifference.

More upsetting to the poet, though, is the Dean's news that one of his contemporaries, Dockery, now has a son at the college. Already feeling a disconcerting sense of exclusion, the poet broods on how young Dockery must have been when he became a father. He drifts into sleep, but when he awakes and changes trains he is still obsessed by the difference between the life of Dockery, a man he can barely recollect, and his own. He is tormented by the thought that the 'High-collared public-schoolboy' made a definite choice about the direction of his life, decided what he wanted from life and achieved it. But such a thought is too challenging to the speaker, too self-belittling, and he retracts it: 'No, that's not the difference. . .'. Self-defensively, he decides that Dockery simply acted on a false premise that 'adding meant increase', whereas to the poet 'it was dilution'. The speaker is drawn on to speculate on the source of our assumptions about the way we should live our lives. We do not act on what we think we ought or want to do, for life simply will not accommodate our most fundamental desires: 'Those warp tight-shut, like doors.' Excluded from our most basic instincts, we are offered by life only the opportunity to fall into habit before we suddenly, and too late, discover that the sum of life has become the accumulation of our habits and routines, that the substance of our existence has become something we never consciously chose. If we stand back from our own lives, we see how we have been caught up and trapped by the 'sand-clouds, thick and close' which have always prevented us from striking out on clear and purposeful directions.

Our lives are smothered in a perpetual, blinding fog which engulfs us whatever faltering steps we make. Hence, there is no essential difference between the poet and Dockery; despite life having brought 'For Dockery a son, for me nothing', neither of them has escaped the imprisoning circumstances of the here and now which allow no possibility of change. Both the ageing bachelor and his opposite, the family man, are subject to the same ungovernable forces:

> Life is first boredom, then fear.
> Whether or not we use it, it goes,
> And leaves what something hidden from us chose,
> And age, and then the only end of age.

Thus, Dockery's fatherhood and the poet's lonely bachelorhood are only superficial differences disguising an essential sameness. Our seeming capacity to choose is one of our most fundamental illusions. We deceive ourselves if we believe that by having acted differently at some crucial point in our past we might have changed our present. The fundamental condition of our lives remains beyond our control; somehow, we seem to have been displaced from our own possibilities, from what might have been, by 'what something hidden from us chose'. Our lives follow an inevitable progression from boredom, through fear, to age and finally death. We are the subjects not of our own choices and decisions, but of the overmastering continuities of time.

Whether or not we are persuaded by the poem's argument is a matter for individual judgement. For the moment, we need to discover how Larkin has created the presence of an individual character and how the poem synthesises anecdotal detail, the swerves and shifts of the speaker's attitude and his abstract reflections into a coherent and moving whole.

Clearly, the visit to his old college is, for the poet, a disappointment. He is uncomfortable in his sober suit, abstractedly nodding dutiful agreement with the Dean. The phrase 'Death-suited' suggests not only his discomposure, but also a cheerless sombreness, as if he is attending the funeral of his own past (he can barely recall having to account for a night's youthful high-spirits, 'unbreakfasted, and still half-tight'). His past is remote, irrecoverable, locked up like his old room. The news, then, that a man who was his contemporary now has a son at the college is a painful reminder of how isolated the speaker is not only from his own past, but from other lives. Tired and rueful, the poet dismisses his college along with 'Canal and clouds'.

But the speaker cannot rid himself of the thought of Dockery. With brilliant economy and accuracy, Larkin catches the tone of mortified self-reproach in 'But Dockery, good Lord,/Anyone up today must have been born/In '43, when I was twenty-one'. Having calculated that Dockery must have become a father at nineteen or twenty, he wearily leaves further speculation in mid-air, 'Well, it just shows/How much . . . How little . . .', before falling asleep. He awakes disgruntled, offended by 'the fumes/And furnace-glares of Sheffield', only to be thrown into deeper petulance by eating 'an awful pie'. In this lingering mood of dissatisfaction, he walks to the end of the platform 'to see the ranged/Joining and parting lines reflect a strong/Unhindered moon'. Larkin manages superbly to combine this factual detail not only with the speaker's mood of embittered loneliness but also with the general theme of the poem. The speaker, in looking at the moonlit railway tracks, is looking at an image of his own life. The tracks take him away from his past at college to a destination which remains always beyond sight. As he stands by the tracks, he is momentarily standing by the side of his own life and trying to assess its direction and the 'Joining and parting lines' act as a reminder of how far his own path has diverged from that of Dockery. Moreover, the direction of his own life, of any life, is as predetermined, as devoid of choice, as the trains which run along these tracks. By contrast, the moon is 'strong/Unhindered', an image of uncomplicated, forthright independence which seems to rebuke our own timid impotence.

With this image for (subconscious) support, then, the speaker can justify himself: 'To have no son, no wife,/No house or land still seemed quite natural'. But he feels an unignorable 'numbness' in recognising how life seems to be passing him by and how his lot seems to be so different from 'the others'. He launches out on an attempt to define the difference between himself and Dockery: notice how Larkin succeeds in capturing the feel of a developing line of thought in 'Dockery, now:/Only nineteen . . .' before it hesitates and collapses in 'No, that's not the difference'. Why does this line of thought stop short of a conclusion? Is it because it would make Dockery seem too determined, too courageous in comparison to the speaker? Certainly, we might think that the speaker begins to load the argument in his own favour when he decides, with an over-zealous semantic scrupulousness, that being 'added to' means 'dilution' rather than 'increase'. What we catch here are the overtly reasonable tones of desperate self-justification. As the speaker moves towards his conclusion that he and Dockery are alike, that he with nothing and Dockery with a son are both subject to a 'harsh patronage', we need to remember that just as the speaker judges Dockery, so we should judge the speaker. We should not take him at face-value: with his rhetorical questions ('Where do these/Innate assumptions come from?') and speculative analogies (is life always like a 'sand-cloud'?), the speaker is himself partial and prejudiced in his views.

Nevertheless, there is a persuasive finality about the final quatrain. It shows once more Larkin's ability to give life and vividness to abstract notions. 'Life is first boredom' because we are caught up in habit, 'then fear' because we realise how inescapably circumscribed and confined by habit we are. Whatever we make of life, 'it goes', leaving us to feel that we were powerless to choose whatever happened to us, that 'something hidden from us' determined our destiny. The language here is remarkably simple and clear, a triumph of poetic technique in articulating complex and inchoate feelings in the diction of ordinariness.

Reference Back

Like 'Triple Time' (in *The Less Deceived*) this poem deals with our subjection to time and the painfulness of memory.

The poet is on a visit home. Bored and dissatisfied, he plays a favourite jazz-record as a temporary distraction, only to hear his mother's inappropriate and banal comment at the end of it: *'That was a pretty one'*. The poet's mood of frustrated discomfort is caught in the repetition of 'unsatisfactory', the mother's nervous attempts to please him and the speaker's lurking guilt at disappointing his mother on a visit to which she had so much looked forward. Once again, the present moment is charged with disappointment both for the speaker (for whom it is 'A time unrecommended by event' as 'Triple Time' puts it) and his mother, who has earlier fallen into the perennial trap of expecting too much of the future (her son's visit home). Henceforth, the poet's favourite blues record will always recall to him this moment when the rift between mother and son became apparent. The record stores up an unhappy memory for the future just as it has stored up 'The flock of notes those antique negroes blew' ever since the record was made thirty years ago. Now, past, present and future are brought by this record into unhappy alignment at the moment when the generation gap between mother and son, her 'unsatisfactory age' and his 'unsatisfactory prime', is suddenly and painfully recognised by them both.

What the poet is made suddenly aware of is time. It is our 'element' because it is the medium in which we have our being, and yet it is also hostile, inhospitable: 'We are not suited to the long perspectives/Open at each instant of our lives'. Every instant of our lives is the product of all preceding instants and the origin of all subsequent ones; every instant is prey to the twin perils of memory and anticipation. The past is beyond recall; the future beyond control. Whether we look forward or backwards we are linked 'to our losses', a lost past or a future beyond our grasp and in which we will continue to lament a lost past that will include this moment. Moreover, because memory preserves our past it presents it to us as it once was, 'Blindingly undiminished', and memory invites us to fall into the delusion that 'By acting differently' we could have kept things as they once were. We are as much pained by resisting that invitation as by accepting it. We are tormented by the activity of time, the constant alteration of future into present into past. Looking back, it always seems that things might now be better had we acted differently, but even there we are deluded, for the present is the consequence of 'what something hidden from us chose' ('Dockery and Son'). We found the same sort of perception in 'Triple Time' which portrayed the past as 'A valley cropped by fat neglected chances/That we insensately forbore to fleece'. Our imaginations possess the painful faculty of simultaneously surveying time's three dimensions: we are conscious of a lost past, of measuring a depleted present against a past idealised by memory, and of the extension of this distressing memorialising into the future.

It is one of the hallmarks of Larkin's poetry that it expresses these rather complex ideas with a simplicity and forcefulness that no paraphrase can match. Notice how many of the words in this poem are simple mono-syllables which express ideas with an easy colloquialism: 'They show us what we have as it once was'. And yet without any sense of strain or dislocation we come upon the more abstract phrase 'Blindingly undi-minished', a brilliant compaction of the abstract 'undiminished', to des-cribe how memory preserves the past intact and whole, and the vivid, energetic word 'Blindingly' which gives us the startling force and glare of those images recollected by memory. We should note as well how the poem's rhyme-scheme shifts from full rhyming couplets to half-rhymes towards the end ('bridge/age...perspectives/lives...worse/was'). This creates an unsettled note as the speaker's reflections become more dis-turbing and also sets up the emphatic full-rhyme ('though/so') at the poem's conclusion as the speaker clinches his argument. The rhyming couplets are muted, however, by the varying rhythms and run-on lines, so that the impression of an informal, speaking voice is preserved.

Wild Oats

This poem exhibits a number of techniques typical of Larkin. First, we see the creation of a character, or persona, who speaks the poem and whose personality emerges from it. Second, the style and language are charac-teristically unobtrusive and colloquial. Finally, the poem deals with Larkin's habitual themes of inadequacy, illusion and disappointment.

The poem's opening is immediately anecdotal, establishing an easy, affable tone of reminiscence: 'About twenty years ago/Two girls came in where I worked'. The speaker relates how he was attracted to the more beautiful girl but courted the plainer friend for a long, uneventful seven years. Eventually, they parted, but it is pictures of the prettier girl which he still keeps in his wallet.

Within the outlines of this simple experience we can perceive a typical Larkinesque persona, a man who seems doomed to fall short of his ideal and to find life passing him by. In a perfect world his 'wild oats' should have been sown with the 'bosomy English rose', whose perfect beauty sparked off 'the whole shooting-match' of sexual desire. Instead, almost inexplicably, it was 'her friend in specs I could talk to' whom he courted. In fact, the explanation is passed over as if too obvious to mention: such beauty is so remote, so unattainable that it must remain only in an ideal dream-world, never actualised. So he goes out with the less attractive girl who, because plainer, belongs more firmly to the world of ordinariness, who does not overwhelm him and who can coexist with him in a mun-dane reality. She is the girl he 'could talk to'. Thus begins a staid, dull courtship that hardens into habit: the dutiful letters and gifts, the routine meetings and finally an indecisive parting. Again, we see the speaker's self-deprecatory insecurity in his rare encounters with the beautiful friend:

'She was trying/Both times (so I thought) not to laugh', where the parenthetical phrase reveals his awed embarrassment. He is condemned to a life of listless dissatisfaction, 'too selfish, withdrawn,/And easily bored to love'. A habit of flippant irony protects him from feeling too deeply: 'Well, useful to get that learnt'. And so the momentos he keeps are of the girl he never knew, a constant reminder of a fulfilment always out of reach. They are 'Unlucky charms', promising not good fortune but the repetition of disappointment.

The everyday language and prosaic style of the poem reinforce our sense of a speaking character relating a familiar experience. The language is plain and idiomatic, involving those everyday words which oil the wheels of conversation: 'I doubt . . . well . . . perhaps'. The use of slang and idiom is barely noticeable: 'bosomy English rose . . . her friend in specs . . . sparked/The whole shooting match off.' The language has the vagueness of conversation: 'About twenty years ago . . . over four hundred letters . . . numerous cathedral cities . . . after about five/Rehearsals'. It is self-mocking in stressing the absurd tedium of the courtship, a courtship which even ends in comic irresolution. The occasional rhyme and loose, three-stress line help to give the impression of a spoken narrative. The final line gains its force not only from the surprising negative ('Unlucky charms') but also from the regularity of its three stresses, its brevity and its rhyme ('snaps . . . perhaps'). This 'sting-in-the-tail' effect is common in Larkin's poetry.

The poem takes up some familiar themes associated with the discrepancy between the ideal and the real. The 'bosomy English rose' embodies a beauty which inspires awe, desire and feelings of unworthiness in the speaker. The phrase itself uses the cliché of a 'rose', but for Larkin clichés can be valuable in summarising common fantasies and feelings (particularly when he negates them, as in 'Unlucky charms', or in 'I Remember, I Remember', the childhood that was 'unspent'). Indeed, the cliché itself keeps the girl remote and unattainable for she never escapes from his conventional responses and stock language: she is simply 'beautiful' and still, at the poem's end, the 'bosomy rose'. She never becomes actual flesh and blood but remains locked in the young man's image of worship. She has no identity except as a symbol of unattainable beauty. The speaker glimpses her only twice more, and on each occasion suspects she is laughing at him, as if beauty itself mocks our inability to transform it into reality. Whether seen in the flesh or in a photograph, the effect is the same in prompting an unsatisfiable yearning. Her 'charms' really are 'Unlucky'. By contrast, her friend 'in specs' belongs, as her blemish suggests, to the real world of drifting discontentment. The speaker can only settle for second-best, and yet this compromise offers no permanent fulfilment.

Essential Beauty

In 'Essential Beauty' Larkin returns to a recurrent symbol of our unattainable desires. Advertisement hoardings, with their huge images of 'how life should be', appeal to our innate sense of beauty, fulfilment and perfection. But experience, 'what happened to happen' ('Send No Money') teaches us that although our imagination can conceive of these ideals, they remain only in the imagination, never transformed into the actual reality of our daily lives. The harder we pursue them, the more quickly they recede from us.

The opening of the poem emphasises the way that these gigantic advertisements, 'In frames as large as rooms', obscure the grim realities of ordinary life: they 'block' streets, 'Screen' graves and 'cover' slums. Their images, 'sharply-pictured' and magnified, camouflage and contrast with the dreariness of urban existence: amongst streets, graveyards and slums they appear as well-ordered and flourishing 'groves'. This pastoral metaphor is exploited by the advertisements themselves with their pictures of a 'silver knife' sinking into 'golden butter', the 'glass of milk' standing in a meadow, all representing in calculated clichés the ideal of a natural, healthy well-being far removed from the reality of urban decay. These images promise everything: contentment, prosperity, even perpetual youth are available in 'that small cube' or the 'cups at bedtime'. Like windows on the world of our dreams, they 'Reflect none of the rained-on streets and squares/They dominate outdoors'. It is as if these advertisements hunt us down with their promises of perfection. Huge, multitudinous, everywhere 'they rise/Serenely to proclaim pure crust, pure foam,/Pure coldness', taunting us with our ideals of flawlessness. And so their images are indeed 'cold', remote from our 'live imperfect eyes' which know the world as tarnished and impure. The billboards depicting 'dark raftered pubs . . . filled with white-clothed ones from tennis-clubs' (an image of social success – notice the mock-reverence of 'white-clothed ones') pretend that reality does not exist, the reality of 'the boy puking his heart out in the Gents'. Reality is what these advertisements cynically overlook (in both senses of the word). The pensioner pays more for his brand of tea only 'To taste old age'.

The poem's final image suggests that these advertisements exploit and painfully reinforce our own fantasies of how things might be in a perfect world. One way in which cigarettes used to be advertised was by explicitly associating smoking with sexual success, thus trading on masculine fears and desires. Larkin uses this image to express the seductiveness and inaccessibility of our dream-images. The 'dying smokers' momentarily sense the object of their desire 'Walking. . . as if on water', miraculous and otherworldly, an 'unfocused she/No match lit up, nor drag ever brought near', a vision of perfection never within reach. And yet the vision is there, 'newly clear,/Smiling, and recognising, and going dark'. It fades, of course, because it is the nature of 'Essential Beauty' to evade us. Our apprehension of it can only ever be transient and fleeting. Larkin is drawn to advertisements as a symbol not just of the discrepancy between the ideal and the real, but as familiar and clichéd projections of our deepest yearnings and desires. When we look at advertisements, we 'stare beyond this world' at a world of ideal perfection, knowing that world to be unavailable to us but not unknowable. We recognise 'that unfocused she' as she briefly recognises us, and Larkin's phrase beautifully combines the vagueness of 'unfocused' with the urgent, sharp simplicity of 'she'. The advertising frames are truly 'rooms that face all ways', not only projecting their images onto us but also revealing to us our own natures.

The poem shows Larkin's command of elaborate and large-scale structures. The sixteen-line stanzas (their bulkiness resembling large advertising frames) are mirror-images, following the same rhyme-scheme (a/b/a/c/b/d/d/e/c/f/e/g/f/h/h/g) with a penultimate three-stress line varying the pentameter. Within this framework, five syntactically complex sentences uncoil. For example, notice how the main verb of the first sentence ('shine') is given its emphasis. First, its position in the sentence is delayed. Secondly, it comes at a point when we expect a rhyme with 'loaves', an expectation which it does not fulfil. Furthermore, the line-ending cuts off the verb from its qualifying adverb ('Perpetually') so that both words are given extra weight. Thus, the verb is given enough force to stand as an ironic contrast to the grim 'streets', 'graves', 'slums' and 'rained-on streets and squares' which actually surround the advertisements. The poem's final line is dramatically effective because of its heavy pauses and rhythmical departure from the prevailing iambic pentameter. It comes as the conclusion to a long final sentence whose rhythm slows and fades with the vision of unreachable beauty.

Afternoons

The poem opens with the suggestion of time passing, of summer drawing to a close, and this sense of decay and decline is developed through the rest of the poem. The poet watches housewives and their children gather each afternoon in the municipal playground and imagines their common experience: marriage, children, the daily routine of housework, the acquisition of household goods. He imagines, too, the uneventful future stretching before them, the repetition of similar afternoons, and concludes with a poignant reflection on our powerlessness in the face of time:

> Their beauty has thickened.
> Something is pushing them
> To the side of their own lives.

What dominates the poem is a melancholy sense of the endless cycle of time, of growth and decay. Summer is 'fading', the leaves falling in 'ones and twos' signifying its barely noticeable passage. This image sets the pattern for the rest of the poem, for in taking up the subject of the women's lives, Larkin sees in them the same natural phenomenon of cyclical growth and decay. These afternoons are described as 'hollows', as if they represent a lull or trough in these women's lives. The children they 'set free' to play are shortly to be 'set free' of them when they launch out on lives of their own and continue the cycle of birth, growth and death. 'Behind' these women stretches the past that has led up to this present, the accumulation of individual experience which is so universal as to be identical. Larkin's description of their past suggests a dull uniformity, a cramped conventionality: marriage, work, domestic routine, material acquisitiveness. The women share a common and equally uneventful future. Before them lie the erosions of time. The wind is 'ruining' their courting-places in a gradual decay, courting-places which are now familiar to the next generation, who will in their turn follow an identical pattern. Their children, 'so intent on/ Finding more unripe acorns' are themselves 'unripe acorns', manifestations of the endless continuity of time. Children and mothers are locked into routine (the children 'Expect to be taken home'), inevitably and inescapably bound by the onward flow of time and a gradual change so slow as to be barely perceptible (like the falling leaves at the poem's opening). The 'new' recreation ground is only momentarily 'new', for like the mothers' courting-places it too will be 'ruined' by the wind of time. The women themselves are suspended in a long, empty ('hollow') interval in their lives: 'Their beauty has thickened'. Youth and beauty have passed, they have given birth to the future generations and now begins the slow decline towards old age and death.

As in 'Dockery and Son' and 'Send No Money' (*'watch the hail/Of occurrence clobber life out/To a shape no one sees'*) Larkin captures with plangent melancholy the sense of an unknowable omnipotence which shapes our lives almost without our knowing it: 'Something is pushing them/To the side of their own lives'. Larkin's language combines simplicity and profundity: the simplicity of the image expresses a complex notion of our own powerlessness in the face of the universal cycle of generation.

An Arundel Tomb

One of Larkin's best-known poems, 'An Arundel Tomb' develops two of his abiding themes: how our individual lives seem rendered virtually redundant by the passage of time and how our human capacity for love cannot triumph over time's destructive force. The poem reveals the masterliness of Larkin's poetic gifts in his ability to control language so as to say things in a way that seems inevitable, moving and true.

The immediate subject of the poem is the monument of a medieval knight and his lady carved on their tomb. We are immediately made aware of time's erosions: their faces are 'blurred', their armour and skirt 'vaguely shown'. The eye travels downward to the feet, where it meets a 'faint hint of the absurd' in the carving of the little dogs underneath. The style of the carving is plain and unadorned ('Baroque' describes a highly ornate and florid style in architecture and music) and there is little to interest us until we notice 'with a sharp tender shock' the earl's left-hand gauntlet held empty in his right hand, leaving his left hand to hold his wife's hand. The third stanza begins on a note of mild cynicism: 'They would not think to lie so long' in real life. This symbol of fidelity 'Was just a detail friends would see', an incidental detail playfully added by the sculptor to support the intended significance of the monument: 'The Latin names around the base'.

At this point in the poem, the tone begins to change. The poet's first cursory glance over the carving has been arrested and he now begins to reflect on the significance of this inconspicuous gesture of the couple's holding hands. For it is this detail in the monument that has best survived the ravages of time: the faces, 'proper habits' and Latin inscription have quickly faded so that 'soon succeeding eyes begin/To look, not read'. The couple could not have anticipated how quickly 'The air would change to soundless damage' as time stealthily erodes the stone and life around them gradually changes. But throughout the long passage of time, the sculpture endures: 'Rigidly they/Persisted, linked, through lengths and breadths/ Of time'. Time has made the couple remote from us, eroding their identity, reducing them 'in the hollow of/An unarmorial age' to historical relics, wispy, vaporous traces of 'their scrap of history'. What remains of them is an 'attitude', a sculpted pose which, sentimentally, we would like to transform into a symbol of undying love. Because that particular detail of the stone sculpture has endured so long, there is a naive temptation to attribute the same endurance to their love for each other. On the contrary, though, 'Time has transfigured them into/Untruth'. Their holding hands, their 'stone fidelity' was, after all, a minor, casual detail, and what was 'hardly meant' has come to be regarded as a deliberate, studied proclamation, 'Their final blazon'. We too eagerly make a comforting equivalence between the survival of their stone hands and the survival of their love. But our *wanting* to make that equivalence, our readiness to make of them a symbol of transcendent love, reveals our need 'to prove/Our almost-instinct almost true:/What will survive of us is love'. Taken in isolation, that last line looks to be optimistic, celebratory. But it is severely qualified: this is our '*almost*-instinct' which the statue proves '*almost* true'. The suggestion here is that it is not quite our instinct to have love survive, for our natures are in truth baser and coarser than that. Similarly, the monument does not quite prove that 'love' survives us and will resist time's obliteration. That is a sentimental misreading.

A study of Larkin's language reveals that this undeceived conclusion is consistent with the rest of the poem. As in 'Talking in Bed', Larkin makes us aware of the pun on 'lie': 'The earl and countess lie in stone' and 'They would not think to lie so long'. The sculptor's 'sweet commissioned grace' (he was, after all, paid to memorialise them) idealises the couple and what he represents in an almost accidental way (it is 'Thrown off') is 'faithfulness in effigy', an image, not real life. Having endured until the present, they have been transfigured into 'Untruth' because in time nothing ultimately survives, neither stone nor love. Their 'fidelity' is, after all, 'stone', cold and inert, an abstraction from real life. The true condition of human life and love is transience, not survival.

And yet Larkin's conclusion is far from cynical. Because the poem is suffused with a plaintive pathos, the conclusion arrives not as an assertion of bitterness and scepticism, but as a hard-won confirmation of the statue's real value and significance. For what the statue preserves is not the couple's names or dates, but the slow passage of time itself. It embodies transience. Larkin's language beautifully and movingly captures the achievement of the memorial: to memorialise, to commemorate, to chronicle time itself. The couple undergo a 'stationary voyage' and Larkin's paradox catches the paradoxical nature of time, its continuity and the permanent state of change. 'Rigidly they/Persisted', and they are 'linked' not only to each other but through history from our own time to theirs, from the present to the past. 'Snow fell, undated. Light/Each summer thronged the glass. A bright/Litter of birdcalls strewed the same/Bone-riddled ground'. In these images, Larkin vividly conveys the sense of time's passage as something creative as well as destructive. 'Undated' suggests how the innumerable snowfalls escape the chronicling of time; the 'thronged' light suggests teeming energy and intensity, and although the ground is 'Bone-riddled', the 'bright/Litter of birdcalls strewed' over it indicates the opulent bountifulness of natural life. The final stanzas, too, emphasise the courtliness of this medieval memorial which is now 'helpless in the hollow of/An unarmorial age' (where 'hollow' has the same force as in 'Afternoons'). 'Transfigured', 'fidelity' and 'blazon', words belonging to a slightly elevated diction, pay tribute to the dignified graciousness of this medieval emblem. The regular rhyme-scheme and iambic tetrameter (four units of unstressed and stressed syllables) reinforce the tone of stately gravity. Within this regularity, though, run-on lines achieve a significant emphasis: 'Rigidly they/Persisted'; 'Time has transfigured them into/Untruth' and in this latter example we see again Larkin's effective and economical use of a surprising negative prefix.

The memorial, then, has persisted, preserving the continuity of time's passage. What will survive us is not love, but time itself as it progresses onwards from us into the future. The conclusion, although unsentimental, is yet far from bleak. In the context of the poem's development, it is consolatory and compassionate. The final line stands as an assertion to which the poet cannot give complete assent. But it represents an ideal which, even if we fall short of it, ennobles us. In a structure of reality that refuses to accommodate our dreams and desires, that is flawed, painful and disillusioning, 'almost' may be the best for which we can hope.

5 CRITICAL DEBATE

The critical response to Larkin's work has generally focused on two broad issues: the view of life expressed in the poems and the nature of his poetic style. These two areas do, of course, largely overlap, for the matter of Larkin's poems and the manner in which it is expressed are interrelated: the lugubriousness of, say, 'Wants' lies as much in the poem's slow, dragging rhythms as in what it actually says.

Larkin has frequently been attacked for his pessimism, a bleakness which sees life as a series of defeats and disappointments. He has been accused of a willed determination to cut down life to its most meagre proportions: life is an accumulation of habits which 'harden into all we've got' and to escape its constricting routines is only to launch oneself into the illusion that the essential conditions of life can be changed. Larkin's supporters would argue that Larkin remained true to his own personal vision and that his duty was to express his own experience as authentically as possible: we cannot blame Larkin if we do not like it. A more profound criticism is that the structure of rationality in Larkin's poems is only a pretence, a mechanism which attempts to disguise the fact that his conclusions are predetermined, that the train of thought which arrives there had its destination planned in advance. In other words, the 'logic' of Larkin's poems is in fact highly partial and prejudiced and not at all the disinterested process of rationalisation it seems to be. Why should it inevitably be the case the 'what/We think truest, or most want to do', as 'Dockery and Son' puts it, 'warp tight-shut, like doors'? That is simply an assertion, not a deduction. The point of this sort of attack is to say that in his poems Larkin does not explore the real possibilities of life but instead carefully nurtures a sense of defeat which refuses to see anything worth celebrating. On the other hand, one might point to a few of Larkin's poems which express an optimism all the more precious because it is hard-won and achieved against all the odds.

A related attack against Larkin is that in deliberately reducing his expectations of life he set out not to challenge or surprise his readers but to court their sympathies, to gain popularity at the expense of real artistry. This is bound up with the criticism that Larkin's poems over the past thirty years have shown little development, that in poem after poem he reasserts the same belittling bleakness with the same techniques and tactics. His themes did not enlarge, his style did not develop and he had nothing to say. Larkin's admirers, though, will point to a growing vigour and toughness in his verse (particularly in his last collection, *High Windows*, published in 1974) and will suggest that in dealing with ideas of free will, time, love and happiness Larkin could hardly be accused of trivialising life.

One recurring criticism made of Larkin, then, is the resignation which his poems so often express. Life is to be tolerated and endured. In his influential anthology, *The New Poetry*, published in 1962, A. Alvarez wittily summed up the typical Larkin persona: 'underfed, underpaid, over-taxed, hopeless, bored, wry . . . he is just like the man next door – in fact, he probably *is* the man next door'. More seriously, Alvarez argued that the poet's resignation represents a dangerous indifference, a complacent gentility which assumes 'that life is always more or less orderly, people always more or less polite, their emotions and habits more or less decent and more or less controllable; that God, in short, is more or less good' (*The New Poetry*, Harmondsworth, Penguin Books, 1962, p. 25). The accusation was that Larkin and other poets associated with him in the Movement, deliberately averted their gaze from urgent contemporary horrors in the world both outside and within us. To the contrary, though, it could be argued that Larkin's quiet, inoffensive tolerance represents the only decent, humane response to the twentieth-century nightmares of the concentration camps and nuclear holocaust. What Alvarez demanded was outrage; what Larkin offers is compassion.

Larkin's poetic style has also aroused controversy. Earlier in the twentieth-century, the leading exponents of modernism (T. S. Eliot and Ezra Pound) introduced a period of radical experimentation in poetry and opened up new possibilities for poetry by exploring the medium of language with energy and daring. In Larkin's poetry, however, there is no hint of that revolution; it is as if he has deliberately refused to profit from any of the poetic innovations made between the two World Wars. His attitude to modernism and experimentation in the arts was well-known: for him it represented a perverse complexity which tries to impress the reader as profundity and cleverness. Larkin's traditional orthodoxy goes hand in hand with his parochialism, a xenophobic reluctance to look beyond the shores of England. Like his friend and admirer, Kingsley Amis, he hated abroad. This is seen by his critics as narrow-mindedness, a refusal to experience anything other than the familiar that is reflected in his style as in his themes. His admirers, though, argue that since Larkin was so thoroughly the master of his own particular style there was no need for him to experiment, and that in any case after a period of upheaval Larkin's poetry represents a necessary retrenchment and a return to tradition.

Despite the controversy, though, there is a general agreement that

Larkin was not only our most popular contemporary poet, but a highly significant one. Although he published comparatively little poetry, his presence will remain major. A comment made by Matthew Arnold on Thomas Gray helps to sum up the range of attitudes to Larkin: 'He is the scantest and frailest of classics in our poetry, but he is a classic'.

REVISION QUESTIONS

1. Choose three poems and analyse the effectiveness in them of Larkin's imagery.

2. Larkin's poems have been described as combining regularity and freedom in their technique. What do you understand by this?

3. Larkin has been criticised for the bleakness and pessimism of his poems. Have you found any reasons to challenge this view in your reading of Larkin?

4. By referring to at least three poems, say what you have found to admire in Larkin's use of language.

5. Discuss the role of nostalgia in Larkin's poetry.

6. Contrast Larkin's attitude to the town and the country as it is shown in his poems.

7. Discuss the effectiveness of Larkin's use of the dramatic monologue.

8. Illustrate the variety of tone in Larkin's poetry.

9. In what ways could any of Larkin's poems be described as 'comic'?

10. 'Condescending and cynical.' Is this how you would describe Larkin's attitude to the characters he creates in his poems?

11. By what means does Larkin illustrate the disparity between reality and illusion in his poems?

12. Discuss the themes of love and time as they are developed in Larkin's poetry.

FURTHER READING

Publications by Philip Larkin

The North Ship (Fortune Press, 1945; 2nd edition with Introduction, Faber & Faber, 1966).
Jill (Fortune Press, 1946; 2nd edition with Introduction, Faber & Faber, 1964).
A Girl in Winter (Faber & Faber, 1947).
XX Poems (privately printed, 1951).
The Less Deceived (Marvell Press, 1955).
The Whitsun Weddings (Faber & Faber, 1964).
All What Jazz? (Faber & Faber, 1970).
High Windows (Faber & Faber, 1974).
Required Writing (Faber & Faber, 1983).

Selected Critical Studies

Bedient, Calvin, 'Philip Larkin', in *Eight Contemporary Poets* (Oxford University Press, 1974).
Davie, Donald, 'Landscapes of Larkin', in *Thomas Hardy and British Poetry* (Routledge & Kegan Paul, 1973).
Haffenden, John, 'Philip Larkin' (interview), in *Viewpoints: Poets in Conversation* (Faber & Faber, 1981).
King, P. R., 'Without illusion: the poetry of Philip Larkin', in *Nine Contemporary Poets* (Methuen, 1979).
Kuby, Lolette, *An Uncommon Poet for the Common Man* (Mouton, 1974).
Martin, Bruce K., *Philip Larkin* (Twayne, 1978).
Motion, Andrew, *Philip Larkin* (Methuen, 1982).
Powell, Neil, 'Philip Larkin: An Uncle Shouting Smut', in *Carpenters of Light* (Carcanet, 1979).

Thwaite, Anthony, 'The Poetry of Philip Larkin', in Martin Dodsworth (ed.) *The Survival of Poetry: A Contemporary Survey* (Faber & Faber, 1970).
Timms, David, *Philip Larkin* (Oliver & Boyd, 1973).

Mastering English Literature

Richard Gill

Mastering English Literature will help readers both to enjoy English Literature and to be successful in 'O' levels, 'A' levels and other public exams. It is an introduction to the study of poetry, novels and drama which helps the reader in four ways - by providing ways of approaching literature, by giving examples and practice exercises, by offering hints on how to write about literature, and by the author's own evident enthusiasm for the subject. With extracts from more than 200 texts, this is an enjoyable account of how to get the maximum satisfaction out of reading, whether it be for formal examinations or simply for pleasure.

Work Out English Literature ('A' level)

S.H. Burton

This book familiarises 'A' level English Literature candidates with every kind of test which they are likely to encounter. Suggested answers are worked out step by step and accompanied by full author's commentary. The book helps students to clarify their aims and establish techniques and standards so that they can make appropriate responses to similar questions when the examination pressures are on. It opens up fresh ways of looking at the full range of set texts, authors and critical judgements and motivates students to know more of these matters.

Also from Macmillan

CASEBOOK SERIES

The Macmillan *Casebook* series brings together the best of modern criticism with a selection of early reviews and comments. Each Casebook charts the development of opinion on a play, poem, or novel, or on a literary genre, from its first appearance to the present day.

GENERAL THEMES

COMEDY: DEVELOPMENTS IN CRITICISM
D. J. Palmer

DRAMA CRITICISM: DEVELOPMENTS SINCE IBSEN
A. J. Hinchliffe

THE ENGLISH NOVEL: DEVELOPMENTS IN CRITICISM SINCE HENRY JAMES
Stephen Hazell

THE LANGUAGE OF LITERATURE
N. Page

THE PASTORAL MODE
Bryan Loughrey

THE ROMANTIC IMAGINATION
J. S. Hill

TRAGEDY: DEVELOPMENTS IN CRITICISM
R. P. Draper

POETRY

WILLIAM BLAKE: SONGS OF INNOCENCE AND EXPERIENCE
Margaret Bottrall

BROWNING: MEN AND WOMEN AND OTHER POEMS
J. R. Watson

BYRON: CHILDE HAROLD'S PILGRIMAGE AND DON JUAN
John Jump

CHAUCER: THE CANTERBURY TALES
J. J. Anderson

COLERIDGE: THE ANCIENT MARINER AND OTHER POEMS
A. R. Jones and W. Tydeman

DONNE: SONGS AND SONETS
Julian Lovelock

T. S. ELIOT: FOUR QUARTETS
Bernard Bergonzi

T. S. ELIOT: PRUFROCK, GERONTION, ASH WEDNESDAY AND OTHER POEMS
B. C. Southam

T. S. ELIOT: THE WASTELAND
C. B. Cox and A. J. Hinchliffe

ELIZABETHAN POETRY: LYRICAL AND NARRATIVE
Gerald Hammond

THOMAS HARDY: POEMS
J. Gibson and T. Johnson

GERALD MANLEY HOPKINS: POEMS
Margaret Bottrall

KEATS: ODES
G. S. Fraser

KEATS: THE NARRATIVE POEMS
J. S. Hill

MARVELL: POEMS
Arthur Pollard

THE METAPHYSICAL POETS
Gerald Hammond

MILTON: PARADISE LOST
A. E. Dyson and Julian Lovelock

POETRY OF THE FIRST WORLD
WAR
Dominic Hibberd

ALEXANDER POPE: THE RAPE OF
THE LOCK
John Dixon Hunt

SHELLEY: SHORTER POEMS &
LYRICS
Patrick Swinden

SPENSER: THE FAERIE QUEEN
Peter Bayley

TENNYSON: IN MEMORIAM
John Dixon Hunt

THIRTIES POETS: 'THE AUDEN
GROUP'
Ronald Carter

WORDSWORTH: LYRICAL
BALLADS
A. R. Jones and W. Tydeman

WORDSWORTH: THE PRELUDE
W. J. Harvey and R. Gravil

W. B. YEATS: POEMS 1919-1935
E. Cullingford

W. B. YEATS: LAST POEMS
Jon Stallworthy

THE NOVEL AND PROSE

JANE AUSTEN: EMMA
David Lodge

JANE AUSTEN: NORTHANGER
ABBEY AND PERSUASION
B. C. Southam

JANE AUSTEN: SENSE AND
SENSIBILITY, PRIDE AND
PREJUDICE AND MANSFIELD
PARK
B. C. Southam

CHARLOTTE BRONTË: JANE EYRE
AND VILLETTE
Miriam Allott

EMILY BRONTË: WUTHERING
HEIGHTS
Miriam Allott

BUNYAN: THE PILGRIM'S
PROGRESS
R. Sharrock

CONRAD: HEART OF DARKNESS,
NOSTROMO AND UNDER
WESTERN EYES
C. B. Cox

CONRAD: THE SECRET AGENT
Ian Watt

CHARLES DICKENS: BLEAK
HOUSE
A. E. Dyson

CHARLES DICKENS: DOMBEY
AND SON AND LITTLE DORRITT
Alan Shelston

CHARLES DICKENS: HARD TIMES,
GREAT EXPECTATIONS AND OUR
MUTUAL FRIEND
N. Page

GEORGE ELIOT: MIDDLEMARCH
Patrick Swinden

GEORGE ELIOT: THE MILL ON
THE FLOSS AND SILAS MARNER
R. P. Draper

HENRY FIELDING: TOM JONES
Neil Compton

E. M. FORSTER: A PASSAGE TO
INDIA
Malcolm Bradbury

HARDY: THE TRAGIC NOVELS
R. P. Draper

HENRY JAMES: WASHINGTON
SQUARE AND THE PORTRAIT OF
A LADY
Alan Shelston

JAMES JOYCE: DUBLINERS AND A
PORTRAIT OF THE ARTIST AS A
YOUNG MAN
Morris Beja

D. H. LAWRENCE: THE RAINBOW
AND WOMEN IN LOVE
Colin Clarke

D. H. LAWRENCE: SONS AND
LOVERS
Gamini Salgado

SWIFT: GULLIVER'S TRAVELS
Richard Gravil

THACKERAY: VANITY FAIR
Arthur Pollard

TROLLOPE: THE BARSETSHIRE
NOVELS
T. Bareham

VIRGINIA WOOLF: TO THE
LIGHTHOUSE
Morris Beja

DRAMA

CONGREVE: COMEDIES
Patrick Lyons

T. S. ELIOT: PLAYS
Arnold P. Hinchliffe

JONSON: EVERY MAN IN HIS
HUMOUR AND THE ALCHEMIST
R. V. Holdsworth

JONSON: VOLPONE
J. A. Barish

MARLOWE: DR FAUSTUS
John Jump

MARLOWE: TAMBURLAINE,
EDWARD II AND THE JEW OF
MALTA
John Russell Brown

MEDIEVAL ENGLISH DRAMA
Peter Happé

O'CASEY: JUNO AND THE
PAYCOCK, THE PLOUGH AND THE
STARS AND THE SHADOW OF A
GUNMAN
R. Ayling

JOHN OSBORNE: LOOK BACK IN
ANGER
John Russell Taylor

WEBSTER: THE WHITE DEVIL AND
THE DUCHESS OF MALFI
R. V. Holdsworth

WILDE: COMEDIES
W. Tydeman

SHAKESPEARE

SHAKESPEARE: ANTONY AND
CLEOPATRA
John Russell Brown

SHAKESPEARE: CORIOLANUS
B. A. Brockman

SHAKESPEARE: HAMLET
John Jump

SHAKESPEARE: HENRY IV PARTS
I AND II
G. K. Hunter

SHAKESPEARE: HENRY V
Michael Quinn

SHAKESPEARE: JULIUS CAESAR
Peter Ure

SHAKESPEARE: KING LEAR
Frank Kermode

SHAKESPEARE: MACBETH
John Wain

SHAKESPEARE: MEASURE FOR
MEASURE
G. K. Stead

SHAKESPEARE: THE MERCHANT
OF VENICE
John Wilders

SHAKESPEARE: A MIDSUMMER
NIGHT'S DREAM
A. W. Price

SHAKESPEARE: MUCH ADO
ABOUT NOTHING AND AS YOU
LIKE IT
John Russell Brown

SHAKESPEARE: OTHELLO
John Wain

SHAKESPEARE: RICHARD II
N. Brooke

SHAKESPEARE: THE SONNETS
Peter Jones

SHAKESPEARE: THE TEMPEST
D. J. Palmer

SHAKESPEARE: TROILUS AND
CRESSIDA
Priscilla Martin

SHAKESPEARE: TWELFTH NIGHT
D. J. Palmer

SHAKESPEARE: THE WINTER'S
TALE
Kenneth Muir

MACMILLAN SHAKESPEARE VIDEO WORKSHOPS

DAVID WHITWORTH

Three unique book and video packages, each examining a particular aspect of Shakespeare's work; tragedy, comedy and the Roman plays. Designed for all students of Shakespeare, each package assumes no previous knowledge of the plays and can serve as a useful introduction to Shakespeare for 'O' and 'A' level candidates as well as for students at colleges and institutes of further, higher and adult education.

The material is based on the New Shakespeare Company Workshops at the Roundhouse, adapted and extended for television. By combining the resources of television and a small theatre company, this exploration of Shakespeare's plays offers insights into varied interpretations, presentation, styles of acting as well as useful background information.

While being no substitute for seeing the whole plays in performance, it is envisaged that these video cassettes will impart something of the original excitement of the theatrical experience, and serve as a welcome complement to textual analysis leading to an enriched and broader view of the plays.

Each package consists of:

* the Macmillan Shakespeare editions of the plays concerned;

* a video cassette available in VHS or Beta;

* a leaflet of teacher's notes.

THE TORTURED MIND
looks at the four tragedies Hamlet, Othello, Macbeth and King Lear.

THE COMIC SPIRIT
examines the comedies Much Ado About Nothing, Twelfth Night, A Midsummer Night's Dream, and As You Like It.

THE ROMAN PLAYS
Features Julius Caesar, Antony and Cleopatra and Coriolanus

THE MACMILLAN SHAKESPEARE

General Editor: PETER HOLLINDALE
Advisory Editor: PHILIP BROCKBANK

The Macmillan Shakespeare features:
* clear and uncluttered texts with modernised punctuation and spelling wherever possible;
* full explanatory notes printed on the page facing the relevant text for ease of reference;
* stimulating introductions which concentrate on content, dramatic effect, character and imagery, rather than mere dates and sources.

Above all, The Macmillan Shakespeare treats each play as a work for the theatre which can also be enjoyed on the page.

CORIOLANUS
Editor: Tony Parr

THE WINTER'S TALE
Editor: Christopher Parry

MUCH ADO ABOUT NOTHING
Editor: Jan McKeith

RICHARD II
Editor: Richard Adams

RICHARD III
Editor: Richard Adams

HENRY IV, PART I
Editor: Peter Hollindale

HENRY IV, PART II
Editor: Tony Parr

HENRY V
Editor: Brian Phythian

AS YOU LIKE IT
Editor: Peter Hollindale

A MIDSUMMER NIGHT'S DREAM
Editor: Norman Sanders

THE MERCHANT OF VENICE
Editor: Christopher Parry

THE TAMING OF THE SHREW
Editor: Robin Hood

TWELFTH NIGHT
Editor: E. A. J. Honigmann

THE TEMPEST
Editor: A. C. Spearing

ROMEO AND JULIET
Editor: James Gibson

JULIUS CAESAR
Editor: D. R. Elloway

MACBETH
Editor: D. R. Elloway

HAMLET
Editor: Nigel Alexander

ANTONY AND CLEOPATRA
Editors: Jan McKeith and
Richard Adams

OTHELLO
Editors: Celia Hilton and R. T. Jones

KING LEAR
Editor: Philip Edwards

MACMILLAN STUDENTS' NOVELS

General Editor: JAMES GIBSON

The Macmillan Students' Novels are low-priced, new editions of major classics, aimed at the first examination candidate. Each volume contains:

* enough explanation and background material to make the novels accessible — and rewarding   to pupils with little or no previous knowledge of the author or the literary period;

* detailed notes elucidate matters of vocabulary, interpretation and historical background;

* eight pages of plates comprising facsimiles of manuscripts and early editions, portraits of the author and photographs of the geographical setting of the novels.

JANE AUSTEN: MANSFIELD PARK
Editor: Richard Wirdnam

JANE AUSTEN: NORTHANGER ABBEY
Editor: Raymond Wilson

JANE AUSTEN: PRIDE AND PREJUDICE
Editor: Raymond Wilson

JANE AUSTEN: SENSE AND SENSIBILITY
Editor: Raymond Wilson

JANE AUSTEN: PERSUASION
Editor: Richard Wirdnam

CHARLOTTE BRONTË: JANE EYRE
Editor: F. B. Pinion

EMILY BRONTË: WUTHERING HEIGHTS
Editor: Graham Handley

JOSEPH CONRAD: LORD JIM
Editor: Peter Hollindale

CHARLES DICKENS: GREAT EXPECTATIONS
Editor: James Gibson

CHARLES DICKENS: HARD TIMES
Editor: James Gibson

CHARLES DICKENS: OLIVER TWIST
Editor: Guy Williams

CHARLES DICKENS: A TALE OF TWO CITIES
Editor: James Gibson

GEORGE ELIOT: SILAS MARNER
Editor: Norman Howlings

GEORGE ELIOT: THE MILL ON THE FLOSS
Editor: Graham Handley

D. H. LAWRENCE: SONS AND LOVERS
Editor: James Gibson

D. H. LAWRENCE: THE RAINBOW
Editor: James Gibson

MARK TWAIN: HUCKLEBERRY FINN
Editor: Christopher Parry